Super Strikers

Ronaldo, Messi, Haaland, Mbappé, and Neymar

Amazing Stories for Kids Aged 8–14

Zach Rosenthal

Table of Contents

INTRODUCTION 1

CHAPTER 1: THE ROOTS OF GREATNESS 5

CHAPTER 2: BREAKTHROUGH MOMENTS 19

CHAPTER 3: DEFINING MATCHES 35

CHAPTER 4: CHALLENGES AND RESILIENCE 47

CHAPTER 5: PEAK PERFORMANCES 61

CHAPTER 6: LEADERSHIP AND INFLUENCE 75

CHAPTER 7: LEGACY AND IMPACT 89

CHAPTER 8: THE FUTURE OF SOCCER 103

CONCLUSION 117

REFERENCES..121

Introduction

Every four years, the world holds its breath as a soccer player steps up to take a crucial penalty kick in the World Cup. In that heartbeat before the foot strikes the ball, that player isn't just representing a country but also becoming a symbol of hope and excitement for fans around the globe. It's in these electrifying moments that ordinary individuals ascend to become legends, etching their names in the hearts of millions and transcending the sport itself.

Soccer isn't just about scoring goals or winning matches; it's about the grit and character of those who play it. It's about players like Lionel Messi, who—despite his humble beginnings in a small Argentine town—rose to global stardom with his incredible perseverance and unmatched skill; or Cristiano Ronaldo, whose dedication and work ethic have made him one of the most well-respected players in the history of the sport. These athletes aren't just masters of the game; they're icons who inspire others to reach for the stars.

This book shares the powerful stories of these soccer giants, telling you about not just their victories and records but also their life stories. Within these pages, we will, in particular, highlight the relentless pursuit of their dreams. Through their journeys, I want to show you that greatness is within your reach if you dare to dream big and work hard.

Each chapter of this book will take you on a journey through the various stages of these players' lives—from their early days kicking a makeshift ball in back alleys to their amazing performances on the world stage. You'll learn not just about their triumphs but also their challenges and how they used these obstacles as stepping stones to greatness.

As a lifelong soccer fan and someone who has faced and overcome many doubts and fears of my own, writing this book was a journey of discovery and passion. I've spent countless hours researching these players to bring you a book that is both inspiring and informative.

Soccer is more than a game; it's a language that bridges continents and cultures, teaching us valuable lessons about teamwork, respect, and perseverance. As you turn these pages, you'll find more than just soccer stories; you'll find a playbook for life.

Get ready to be inspired, to learn, and to see soccer in a way you never have before. You're about to embark on an unforgettable adventure into the lives of the greatest soccer players of our time. Let's kick off this journey together, and who knows? Maybe one day, your name will be the one inspiring the next generation of players.

Chapter 1:

The Roots of Greatness

Have you ever wondered where legends begin? It's not in the bright lights of a packed stadium or the roar of a crowd when a goal hits the back of the net; a person's path to greatness starts way before that, in the quiet corners of their small town and the dusty fields where a future star learns to kick a ball. This chapter is like opening up an old family album, flipping back to the first few pages where the pictures are a bit faded but the stories they tell are pure gold. First, we'll delve into the beginnings of one such legend: Lionel Messi. His journey from a little kid with a big dream in Rosalio, Argentina to a global soccer icon is nothing short of epic. So, lace up your boots. We're taking a trip down memory lane to where it all started!

Messi's Humble Beginnings in Rosario

Family Influence

In the bustling city of Rosario, Argentina, nestled within the tight embrace of his family, Lionel Messi took his first steps toward greatness. But it was his grandmother, Celia, who first saw the spark of future greatness in little "Leo." She would accompany him to training and matches, cheering the loudest and making sure he never missed a practice. Messi himself has often said that he owes a lot to his grandmother. She was the one who truly nurtured his passion for the game. Her belief in him wasn't just a gentle push; it was the wind beneath his wings, propelling him toward the soccer stratosphere. She was the one who pushed the manager of his local team to let him play, even when he was too young for any of the regional age categories. This deep, familial support provided Messi with a foundation stronger than concrete—a base from which he could leap toward his dreams.

Health Challenges

However, Messi's path to glory wasn't just lined with cheers and goals; it also had its hurdles, most notably his battle with a growth hormone deficiency that was diagnosed when he was just 11. The treatment was pricey—a towering financial burden for a middle-class family. Imagine being that young and having to face daily injections and the uncertainty of your future in the sport you love! Yet, it was this very challenge that shaped Messi's unyielding resilience and determination. He saw each injection, each treatment, as a step toward his dream, which is a shining testament to his resolve not to let anything—not even his own body—keep him from the game that gave him so much joy.

Early Recognition of Talent

Messi's talent was undeniable, even as a boy. At the age of just five, he began playing for a local club coached by his father, swiftly moving on to play for Newell's Old Boys.

Here, in the youth leagues, Messi was not just participating; he was dominating, playing against children who were often significantly bigger than him. He had a way of moving with the ball that seemed almost magic, mesmerizing those who watched. Imagine a tiny kid, weaving through a forest of legs twice his size, with a soccer ball that seemed glued to his feet. It was in these early days that Messi showed signs of the future champion he would become.

Overcoming Adversity

The most pivotal moment, however, came when Messi's talent outgrew the resources available in his hometown. His need for advanced treatment and better soccer training prompted a bold decision: moving to Barcelona. This was no small feat; it involved uprooting his entire life for a chance at a potential future in soccer. It was a gamble that carried the weight of immense risk; failure would mean not just financial ruin but also crushing his young dreams. Yet, with the support of his family, Messi moved to Spain, joining the youth academy at FC Barcelona. This move was the catapult that launched his career, proving that, sometimes, taking the biggest risk leads to the greatest reward.

In these early chapters of his life, we can see not just the making of a great athlete but the shaping of his resilient spirit. Messi's story teaches us that behind every kick, every goal, and every trophy, there's a story of struggle, support, and the relentless pursuit of dreams. As we turn the pages from his past to his present, it will become even more clear that greatness isn't just about what you achieve but what you overcome to get there. For now, let's look at the history of another soccer legend.

Cristiano Ronaldo's Youth in Madeira and Sporting Lisbon

Have you ever wondered how a kid from a small island in the middle of the ocean could become one of the biggest stars in the world of soccer? Well, Cristiano Ronaldo's story starts in Madeira, Portugal—a place known more for its rugged landscapes and wine than for fútbol prodigies. Growing up in a tiny, tin-roofed home—the kind where you could hear the rain tap-dancing overhead—Ronaldo's family wasn't exactly swimming in riches. They were a tight-knit group, working hard just to keep the lights on.

This modest beginning wasn't a setback, though; it was the fuel that fired up Ronaldo's ambition. From a young age, he learned the value of hard work by watching his family juggle multiple jobs. Yet, he also knew that life wasn't just about making ends meet; it was about chasing a dream so big that it would take them out of the hardship they knew all too well. Imagine being barely old enough to go to Kindergarten and already having the determination to wake up every day with one goal in mind: to play fútbol.

Ronaldo's journey to greatness kicked off at Andorinha, where his dad worked as a kitman. Here, he wasn't just playing the game; he was laying down the foundation of his work ethic, practicing till the sun dipped below the horizon. But the real test came when he moved to Nacional, one of Madeira's top fútbol clubs. It was here that Ronaldo first tasted the bitter flavor of loneliness, miles away from the warmth of his family. This chapter of his life was like stepping into a big, scary world all alone, armed with nothing but a ball and a dream.

The saga took an even more exciting turn when Ronaldo, at the age of just 12, packed his bags for Lisbon, joining Sporting's prestigious youth academy. Picture this young kid, navigating a new city and a new language—yes, Madeirans speak Portuguese, but the Lisbon dialect can be another beast! And this was all going down while he was trying to prove he was the best among a crowd of hopefuls.

It was at Sporting Lisbon that Ronaldo's talent started shining brighter than a lighthouse on a foggy night. His skills on the field grew exponentially, fueled by a blend of natural talent and a relentless drive to improve. Coaches at the academy couldn't stop talking about his lightning speed, his jaw-dropping dribbles, and that trademark rocket of a shot that would later become feared by goalkeepers all over the world.

But let's zoom in on one particularly game-changing moment: During a match against a team packed with top young talents, Ronaldo was auditioning for the big leagues. Each dribble and each step-over was a statement saying, "Here I am, world; ready or not!" And boy, did he nail it! His performance was so electrifying that it buzzed through the stands, all the way into the ears of the first-team coaches. Before he knew it, Ronaldo was called up to join Sporting's senior squad, setting the stage for a career that would later see him jetting off to Manchester United and then becoming a global icon.

In these early years, Ronaldo was more than just a kid with a ball. He was a force of nature, reshaping every challenge into a stepping stone toward greatness. His story teaches us that where you come from doesn't decide where you end up. Whether it's a small island in the Atlantic or a sprawling city, greatness starts with a dream and a whole lot of determination.

Neymar's Early Years in Santos

Imagine stepping into a world where soccer flows in the veins of the people just as naturally as the rhythm of samba beats on a Brazilian beach. For Neymar da Silva Santos Júnior, this wasn't just a dreamy backdrop; it was the reality of growing up in a home where soccer was more than a game; it was also a family legacy. Neymar's dad— a former professional soccer player—was both a coach and a mentor right in their backyard. This early exposure to the beautiful game sparked a fiery love in young Neymar, who would dribble and dash around with a ball from the moment he could walk.

At the tender age of 11, Neymar stormed into Santos FC with the force of a mini hurricane. From the get-go, his raw talent was undeniable. Santos FC wasn't just any club; it was the nurturing ground for soccer greats like Pelé. Here, Neymar was sculpting his future with every kick and flick of the ball.

The coaches at Santos saw something special in him: His dribbles were sharper, his sprints faster, and his goals... Oh, the goals were just spectacular! His training at such a young age wasn't merely about learning the ropes; it was about weaving those ropes into a net that would one day catch his dreams.

Neymar's style on the field was as bold and distinct as a graffiti-tagged wall in downtown São Paulo. He brought a sense of swagger to the game that was all his own, marked by bold dribbles and a flair for dramatic finishes.

Santos FC's youth setup was the perfect canvas for Neymar. The coaches there didn't just tolerate his showy style; they encouraged it. They knew that within this young boy's fancy footwork lay the heart of Brazilian soccer—a blend of skill, joy, and an unapologetic flair for the dramatic. Neymar turned each match into a mini-carnival, where spectators would often find themselves gasping, cheering, and dancing to the rhythm of his moves.

But it wasn't all smooth sailing. During his early years, Neymar Júnior was noticeably smaller and less imposing than many of his peers—a challenge that often plays on a young athlete's mind and body. However, what Neymar lacked in size, he more than made up for in speed and smarts. His agility was his secret weapon; he could change directions like a swift wind, leaving bigger and stronger defenders tangled in their own legs. It was a classic case of David versus Goliath, except this David didn't need a sling; his weapon was a soccer ball at his feet.

In those days, Santos FC's training ground was where Neymar honed his knack for turning physical limitations into advantages—a lesson in using our perceived weaknesses as strengths. His ability to outmaneuver opponents who towered over him taught him resilience and gave him a deeper understanding of the game. Neymar's early years at Santos laid the tracks for a journey that was destined to be extraordinary, driven by the pure, undiluted passion of a boy who was born to play soccer. As he grew in skill and stature, so too did his influence on the field, turning every Santos match into an anticipation of what magic Neymar would conjure next.

Mbappé's Ascent from Bondy to Monaco

Picture a small suburb just a stone's throw from the bustling streets of Paris: Welcome to Bondy, where the vibrant energy of the city meets the tight-knit community vibes of the suburbs. This is where Kylian Mbappé's story begins—not amidst the glamor of a big city but in a place marked by its socioeconomic challenges. Bondy might not be the first place you'd think of when you imagine the birthplace of a future soccer superstar, but it's where Kylian found his first ball and kicked it with dreams bigger than those challenges.

Growing up in Bondy, life was about navigating the realities of an area striving for more. Yet, in this environment, Kylian's family created a sanctuary that was all about sports. His dad, Wilfried, wasn't just a fútbol coach; he was a guiding force in Kylian's life. Imagine having a coach 24/7, ready to drill you in the tactics of life and fútbol— that was Kylian's dad. And his mom, Fayza was a former professional handball player who brought her own fierce competitiveness and sports insights to the dinner table. This blend of discipline, love for sports, and a constant push to excel formed the backbone of Mbappé's early training ground.

From the moment young Kylian started kicking a ball in the local fields of AS Bondy, it was clear he was different. It wasn't just his speed that made spectators and coaches do a double take—although, let's be honest, he could probably outrun a cheetah on a good day. What really set him apart was his fútbol intelligence—his uncanny ability to read the game and make decisions that players twice his age would hesitate over. Kylian darted through the youth ranks like a comet, lighting up every match with his brilliance and leaving a trail of awed onlookers in his wake.

The real turning point came when he moved to the prestigious Clairefontaine academy—France's hotbed for fútbol prodigies. Picture this: a place where the best of the best gather, where every training session feels like a World Cup match, and where every player dreams of becoming the next big thing in French fútbol. At Clairefontaine, Kylian wasn't just another hopeful; he was a standout star. His time at the academy taught him how to prepare to shine on the bigger stage and ready himself for the challenges of professional fútbol.

And shine he did! His next leap from Clairefontaine to Monaco was like doing a high dive—thrilling and a bit terrifying. But Kylian wasn't just ready; he was raring to go. At Monaco, he quickly became the player to watch. His debut as a professional player came when he was barely old enough to drive, but on the field, he drove through defenses with the ease of a seasoned pro.

But it wasn't until a match against Manchester City in the Champions League that Kylian truly announced himself to the world. That night, under the bright lights of the European stage, Mbappé dazzled, scoring goals and showcasing a level of skill that had the top clubs across Europe sitting up and taking notice.

In those early days at Monaco, Kylian's life changed rapidly. He wasn't just a promising player; he was a headline-maker, a record-setter, and a beacon of hope for many young athletes back in Bondy. His rise was meteoric, filled with the kind of moments that young players dream of. But through it all, he remained grounded—a kid from a suburb near Paris who dared to dream big, backed by a family that believed those dreams could be a reality. As he tore up the pitch at Monaco, it was clear that Mbappé was on a path to greatness, not just because of his talent but also because of his relentless drive—a trait honed on the fields of Bondy and polished at Clairefontaine.

Haaland's Norwegian Roots and His Move to Molde

Imagine a small, quiet town in Norway, where the winters are long and the fútbol fields are often covered in snow. This is Bryne, where kids play fútbol not just for fun but with the hope of becoming the next big star. In this chilly corner of the world, Erling Haaland first kicked a soccer ball, spurred on by his dad, Alf-Inge Haaland, who was himself a professional soccer player.

Growing up in such a sporty household, it was almost like Erling was destined to follow in his father's footsteps. But unlike other kids who might feel pressured, Erling took to fútbol like a duck to water—or maybe, like a Viking to exploration; it was adventurous, thrilling, and downright fun.

From a very young age, Erling's talent was as clear as a Norwegian fjord. He joined his local club, Bryne FK, and it wasn't long before he began to stand out, not just for his height but for his incredible ability to score goals. You could say he was like a young tree, growing taller and stronger right before everyone's eyes, and as he grew, so did his reputation.

Imagine a young lad, towering over others, sprinting down the field like a gazelle, and hitting the ball so hard it would make the net shiver. That was Haaland, making waves in the youth leagues by showing not just physical growth but a knack for finding the back of the net with astonishing regularity.

The buzz around his talent grew louder, and soon, it was time for a bigger stage. His move to Molde—under the watchful eyes of Ole Gunnar Solskjaer—was like turning the page to an exciting new chapter of his life. Molde wasn't just any club; it was a place known for polishing raw talents into gleaming gems. Under Solskjaer—a legend at Manchester United and a revered figure in Norwegian fútbol—Haaland found not just a coach but a mentor. Solskjaer's guidance was like a map for a treasure hunter, showing Erling the paths to take, the traps to avoid, and the shortcuts to success. There, his training intensified, the stakes were higher, and every match was a test—a chance to prove himself.

Then came the breakout season that would etch his name into the minds of fútbol fans everywhere. It was at Molde that Haaland's potential began to turn into performance. Each match was a display of his growth, not just as a player but as a professional. He wasn't just scoring goals; he was outsmarting seasoned defenders with his movements and displaying a calmness in front of the goal that belied his age. His ability to read the game, to be in the right place at the right time, and to finish with a cold precision made him a standout player, not just on his team but in the league as a whole.

This local kid from a small town was now the talk of the nation, scoring goals that were replayed on screens all across the country and even catching the eyes of clubs across Europe. His performances were like a series of loud knocks on the doors of the fútbol world—each goal a statement, each match a step towards something bigger.

But what made Erling's rise even more impressive was his humility and work ethic. Despite the spotlight, he remained grounded, playing the game he loved, enjoying every moment, and working even harder to improve. His journey at Molde set the stage for what was to come, showing us that no matter where you start, with the right attitude and guidance, the sky's the limit. And for Erling Haaland, this was just the beginning.

Chapter 2:

Breakthrough Moments

Alright, strap in, because we're about to zoom into some seriously epic moments that turned talented youngsters into soccer legends. Think of it like the first time you beat that really tough level on your favorite video game; suddenly, you felt invincible, right? Well, that's kind of what these breakthrough moments did for our soccer heroes, proving that they could play in the big leagues and totally changing the game, both for them and for us fans!

Messi's First League Title With Barcelona

Catalyst for Confidence

Picture this: The year is 2004, and a young Lionel Messi, who's just a teenager, is playing for one of the biggest clubs in the world, FC Barcelona. Winning a league title with such a club sounds like a dream for any player, right? But for Messi, it was more than just a trophy to put on his shelf; it was the golden ticket that really kicked off his career. Scoring in those crucial matches and helping his team clinch the La Liga title was like Messi telling the world, "Hey, I'm here, and I'm not just a benchwarmer!"

Winning that title as a youngster injected a mega boost of confidence into Messi. It was like flipping a switch; he went from "Messi, the promising kid" to "Messi, the key player." Despite being such a young lad, he was suddenly trusted to deliver results in high-pressure games, and even better, he was actually pulling it off!

This pivotal moment proved to Messi himself, and to everyone else, that he was ready to play with the big boys. It set a fire under him, pushing him to dive headfirst into his career, hungry for more victories and ready to carve out a name for himself in the soccer hall of fame.

Impact on Playing Style

With his confidence levels hitting new heights, Messi started taking more risks on the field. Before this breakthrough, he was already a nifty player, but now, he began to add more flair and boldness to his game. You know those crazy dribbles and stunning goals we all gawk at in highlight reels? Those started becoming more frequent at this point in his budding career. Messi began to assert himself more during games, taking on defenders with a cheeky confidence that said, "I got this."

This transformation was crucial. It wasn't just about showing off his skills; Messi was adapting his play to take on more responsibility within the team. He started evolving from a talented youngster to a pivotal playmaker who could change the course of a game with a single move. This shift not only spiced up Barcelona's attacks but also made watching their games a treat for soccer fans around the globe. Who doesn't love seeing someone who plays with a bit of swagger, right?

Team Dynamics

Now, let's chat about the squad: The Barcelona team's dynamics played a massive role in shaping young Messi, especially his relationship with soccer maestro Ronaldinho. Imagine having one of the world's best players as your mentor! Ronaldinho wasn't just a teammate; he was like the cool big brother Messi looked up to. He took Messi under his wing, showing him the ropes both on and off the pitch and teaching him how to handle fame and pressure while still having a blast playing soccer.

This mentorship was key in helping Messi gel with the team and understand the rhythm of top-tier soccer. It's one thing to be skilled, but understanding how to sync those skills with other world-class talents? That's what sets a legendary player apart from a great one. Ronaldhino's guidance helped Messi fit into the complex puzzle that is a championship-winning team, making their plays smoother, more intuitive, and frankly, a joy to watch.

Media and Public Perception

Before the league win, Messi was already on the public's radar, but he was often seen as just another promising young talent. Post-victory, the media and public perception of him shifted dramatically. Now, his potential was exploding into reality. Messi started being touted not just as a future star but as a current leading light, crucial to his team's success.

This shift in perception was massive. The spotlight was now firmly on Messi. This meant that expectations for him were set sky-high, but it also came with a newfound respect from fans and critics alike. His jersey started flying off the shelves, and kids around the world were sticking posters of him on their walls, dreaming of dribbling like Messi. This was the moment that catapulted him from a youngster to watch to a global icon in the making.

And there you have it: the chapter in Messi's life that turned him from a hopeful kid into a soccer powerhouse. As we dive deeper into these moments, remember, it's not just about the glory; it's also about the journey, the growth, and the sheer joy of playing soccer. And who knows? Maybe, you're a future soccer legend, oozing potential even as you're reading this right now. So, keep playing, keep dreaming, and maybe, one day, I'll be writing about your breakthrough moment!

Ronaldo's Game-Changing Season at Manchester United

Back in the 2006–07 season, Cristiano Ronaldo was making waves bigger than those of the coast of his home island of Madeira. Picture this: You're at Old Trafford, the crowd is buzzing, and there's Ronaldo, not just playing fútbol but redefining what it means to be a winger at one of the world's most famous fútbol clubs, Manchester United.

This wasn't just any season; it was the one where Ronaldo transformed from a promising player to a headline-grabbing superstar. His stats were off the charts—scoring goals, dishing out assists, and just generally causing mayhem for defenders. Every match was a chance to expect the unexpected. Ronaldo was not just part of the team; he was becoming the heart of it, pumping adrenaline with every dribble, every free kick, and every thunderous goal.

Ronaldo's skills with the ball were like something out of a video game. This season saw him level up his dribbling and free-kick techniques. Remember those jaw-dropping, swerving free kicks? Yep, Ronaldo turned those into an art form this season. Seeing his dribbling was like watching someone dance while keeping a balloon away from a horde of toddlers. Defenders knew what he was going to do, but they just couldn't stop it.

It was during this season that Ronaldo perfected the "chop"—that quick flick of the ball behind his leg followed by a change in direction. Was it simple? Maybe. Effective? Absolutely! Each game displayed that Ronaldo's toolbox of skills was growing more formidable, making him not just a player to keep an eye on but *the* player to watch.

But hey, it wasn't just about physical skills. Mentally, Ronaldo was on another level. This season was like a master class in mental toughness. Playing at such a high level for one of the world's most scrutinized clubs brings pressure that can crush even seasoned pros. But Ronaldo thrived on it. He transformed pressure into performances that left fans and critics alike in awe.

His ability to seize control of games during crucial moments was becoming his trademark. Whether it was stepping up for a tie-breaking penalty or rocketing a free kick into the net from 30 yards out, Ronaldo displayed a leadership quality on the pitch that resonated with fans and inspired his teammates. This mental growth was pivotal, not just for his game but for his entire career. It set the foundation for the leader he would become, both on and off the field.

As the season wrapped up, the praise started rolling in. Ronaldo's trophy cabinet started to fill up with personal awards alongside team honors. His performances earned him the Premier League's Player of the Season and the FIFPRO World Player of the Year, among others. Each award was a nod to his excellence and proof of how his hard work was paying off. These weren't just trophies to collect dust; they were confirmations that Ronaldo had elevated his game to be among the best in the world. He wasn't just being a great player; he was becoming a global icon, setting standards for what it means to be a professional in the modern game.

This season was a defining chapter in Ronaldo's story—a period that showcased his evolution from a talented youngster to a fútbol superstar known across the globe. His blend of skill, determination, and the ability to perform under the brightest lights was what made this season not just memorable but legendary. As we look back, it's clear that this was the beginning of Ronaldo's era—a time in which he was changing the game, one goal at a time.

Neymar's Breakout Performance in the 2011 South American Cup

Have you ever had one of those days when everything you do just turns to gold? Well, Neymar had something like that back in 2011, but it wasn't just a day; it was the whole South American Cup! In this tournament, Neymar played like he was from another planet, dazzling fans and baffling defenders with his mind-blowing skills. It was in this high-stakes competition that Neymar truly stepped up, turning the soccer field into his own personal stage and transforming Santos FC's march to victory into a highlight reel of his burgeoning talents.

Neymar's performance during this tournament was nothing short of a soccer symphony. Every touch of the ball was a note played perfectly, every dribble a melody, and every goal a crescendo. Picture this: Neymar, with the ball at his feet, facing down a defender. With a swift flick and a burst of speed, he's past his marker, leaving them grasping at air. It's just him and the goalkeeper now. With a cool calmness that ignores the roaring crowd around him, he slots the ball into the back of the net. Goal! But Neymar wasn't just focused on scoring; his assists were equally spectacular, turning over goal-scoring opportunities with a vision so sharp it could cut glass. This wasn't just a player having a good run; this was Neymar announcing himself as a force to be reckoned with.

But what truly set this tournament apart for Neymar was how it showcased his ability to perform under the glaring spotlight of expectation. Santos FC carried the weight of a glorious history, and Neymar, with his dazzling play, shouldered that history with a flair that had fans on the edge of their seats. Sure, that came with added pressure, but Neymar danced around it just as easily as he did around opposing defenders. This ability to shine when the stakes were highest was an impressive sign of a player who was ready to take the next big leap in his career.

Additionally, seeing Neymar's leadership growth during this tournament was like watching a young prince grow into a king. He wasn't just a player; he was a leader on the pitch, driving his team forward with as much passion as skill. You could see him rallying his teammates, urging them on. His energy was infectious, his determination unyielding. Neymar was taking charge, taking responsibility, and taking his team to new heights. It was during these moments that he transitioned from a prodigious talent to a leader, not just by wearing the captain's armband but also by inspiring those around him to rise to the occasion.

And rise they did, all the way to victory, and clubs across Europe were sitting up to take notice. Neymar's performances put him squarely on the radar of the biggest clubs in the world, each eager to bring this South American sensation to their squad. The buzz was unavoidable, the excitement palpable. Here was a player who could change the fortunes of a team—whose skills promised not just goals but also ticket sales, jerseys flying off shelves, and a spike in fans.

Neymar's masterclass in the 2011 South American Cup didn't just win him a trophy; it won him a place on the grand stages of European fútbol, setting the stage for his eventual move to Barcelona, where the bright lights awaited his magic and the fans awaited their new hero. This tournament was more than just a collection of matches; it was Neyval's stepping stone to becoming a global fútbol icon.

Mbappé's Role in Monaco's League Triumph

Imagine being a teenager and not just playing for a top-tier European fútbol club but actually becoming a pivotal piece in winning a major league title. It sounds like something out of a sports movie, right? Well, for Kylian Mbappé, this was his real life during the 2016–17 season with AS Monaco.

This was the season that saw Monaco dethrone giants and grab the Ligue 1 title, and young Mbappé was right at the heart of it all. His role? Oh, just leading the attacks, scoring bucketloads of goals, and running defenses ragged. No big deal, just typical teenage stuff!

Mbappé's impact that season was like dropping a turbocharged engine into a classic car. Suddenly, Monaco wasn't just going; they were flying. His ability to find the back of the net was uncanny. Picture this: The ball rolls to Mbappé's feet, there's a palpable pause in the air, and in a blink, he's around his marker and shooting past the goalkeeper. It was this scoring prowess that saw him netting a whopping *26 goals* across all competitions, making him the threat to watch out for. Each of those goals was a statement, loud and clear, that he was a star burning bright and fast, and everyone better pay attention.

But Mbappé wasn't just a goal machine. His tactical versatility made him a nightmare for any defense. Monaco's coach, Leonardo Jardim, utilized Mbappé's speed and intelligence in fascinating ways. Sometimes, he'd play on the wings, using his blistering pace to break through defensive lines and create chances. Other times, he'd be in the center, right in the thick of the action, using his quick feet and sharp instincts to pivot past defenders and shoot. He was about strategically deployed like a dynamic weapon all over the field to outsmart opponents. This tactical flexibility not only showcased Mbappé's diverse skill set but also kept every opponent guessing, never quite sure how Monaco would unleash their young star next.

Now, add to this mix Mbappé's youthful exuberance—that fearless, all-in energy of a young star who plays like he has nothing to lose. There's something infectious about a young talent playing with unbridled joy and fearlessness; it can light up a whole team. And he definitely did light up Monaco!

His enthusiasm and relentless energy had a ripple effect on the team, often lifting the spirits and performances of his more experienced teammates. It's one thing to have skill, but to inspire a squad of seasoned professionals as a teenager? That's something special. Mbappé's presence brought a fresh, vibrant energy to Monaco's play, making their games particularly exciting to watch.

The climax of this roller-coaster season—lifting the Ligue 1 trophy—was a launchpad for Mbappé's career on the international stage. His outstanding performances caught the eyes of the world, and soon, he was not just a national sensation but a global one. It was this breakthrough season that catapulted him into the national team, setting him up for his debut and subsequent rise in French fútbol.

Each game he played was like an audition on the world stage, and boy, did he land the part. From here, there was no looking back. This young man from Bondy was now on the fast track to becoming a global superstar, all thanks to a season that read like the perfect script for a sports blockbuster.

So, as you flip through these pages, remember that this time in Mbappé's life shows us what youthful spirit—when guided with the right tactics and unleashed with fearless joy—can achieve. It's about making every moment on the field count, playing not just to win but to inspire. And for Mbappé, this was just the beginning.

Haaland's Dominance in the U-20 World Cup

Imagine stepping onto the pitch, the crowd buzzing with anticipation, and then blowing everyone's minds by scoring not one, not two, but *nine* goals in a single match. That's exactly what Erling Haaland did at the U-20 World Cup against Honduras in 2019. This was a record-smashing performance that sent shockwaves around the soccer world. This young Norwegian striker, tall and powerful, moved with a grace that was unexpected for his size, making the extraordinary look effortless. Each of those nine goals not only showcased his raw talent but also gave audiences across the globe a sneak peek into the soccer phenomenon he was destined to become.

This epic game was a display of Haaland's technical prowess and physical dominance. His ability to be in the right place at the right time—which seems like a simple skill—is actually a complex blend of quick thinking, sharp instincts, and relentless energy that have always made him a force to be reckoned with on the field.

And let's talk about his finishing: Oh boy, whether it was a delicate tap-in, a thunderous shot from outside the box, or a sneaky header, at the U-20 World Cup, Haaland demonstrated that he could score from anywhere at any time. His physical strength also meant he could shrug off defenders as if they were just pesky flies, maintaining composure where others might falter.

But scoring goals wasn't the only thing Haaland was doing; he was also sending a message to the soccer community worldwide. This performance put Haaland squarely on the radar of big European clubs. Scouts and managers sat up a little straighter, their eyes wide, their minds racing, all thinking the same thing: *We need him*. Haaland's dominance at this international youth level was his formal introduction to the world—a loud and clear declaration of his readiness to take on bigger challenges in more competitive leagues.

The skills Haaland displayed during this tournament were a clear indicator of his potential to succeed at the highest levels of soccer. His positioning, for instance, is a skill that might not grab headlines like a flashy dribble or a long-range goal, but it's crucial. Being in the right spot at the right time is about reading the game, understanding opponent movements, and predicting where the ball is going to be. This spatial awareness is what often separates the good players from the great ones.

Then, there's his finishing ability—a skill that seems simple yet is anything but. The composure and precision Haaland showed against Honduras—whether the goal was a simple tap-in or a complex volley—demonstrated a maturity beyond his years and a sharpness that would terrify any goalkeeper.

These remarkable abilities didn't just enhance his reputation; they also significantly influenced transfer decisions. Clubs were eager, possibly even desperate, to have such a talent on their roster. This wasn't about potential anymore; it was about proven skill and the certainty that Haaland could bring his goal-scoring prowess to their team and replicate this breathtaking performance against tougher opponents in more challenging environments.

The impact of his performance at the U-20 World Cup was profound, setting the stage for his next big move, which would eventually see him joining Borussia Dortmund—a club known for polishing young talents into world-class stars. Here, Haaland wouldn't just be another player; he was going to be the player to watch, expected to bring his record-breaking scoring ability to one of Europe's top leagues.

As we wrap up this chapter, it's clear that any significant victory is not just a breakout moment; it's also a bold statement of intent. From a player's technical skills and physical prowess to their mental resilience and quick thinking on the field, having a well-rounded skill set at a young age is what opens the capacity to be not just a fleeting wonder but a rising star poised to shine on the global stage. Each success is a thrilling snapshot of what determination, skill, and raw power can achieve when perfectly combined on the soccer field. As we move forward, the excitement only builds, leaving us all looking forward to just how high these stars will soar in the chapters to come.

Chapter 3:

Defining Matches

Now, we're diving into some of the most jaw-dropping, cheer-sparking, and downright legendary matches that have turned these amazing players into soccer icons! Think of these moments as those big, booming fireworks at the end of a show that leave you saying, "Wow, did that just happen?!" These are where our favorite players stepped up and showed the world exactly what they're made of.

Messi's Solo Goal Against Getafe Compared to Maradona

Iconic Goal Analysis

Picture this: It's 2007, and a young Lionel Messi is about to do something so spectacular that it gets its own place in soccer history. We're talking about that Copa del Rey semifinal against Getafe, where Messi played like he was from another planet.

Now, if you're a soccer fan, you might know about Diego Maradona's "Goal of the Century" in the 1986 World Cup. Well, Messi's goal was like watching a live replay of that!

Starting from his own half, he dodged and weaved through not one, not two, but *five* Getafe players before coolly slotting the ball past the keeper. It was like watching a magician pulling off the world's greatest trick!

The reason why this goal was so talked about wasn't just the beauty of it but the eerie similarity to Maradona's famous goal—both legends wearing that iconic number 10 jersey, showcasing their dribbling skills, and scoring in a crucial match. And in Messi's case, this goal screamed, "Hey, I might just be the next big thing in soccer!"

Technical Skill Display

Let's break down the magic: First, there's the dribbling, done at full speed, dodging tackles left and right. Messi's control of the ball was so tight that it was as if the ball was glued to his feet. Then, there's the speed. Messi was like a mini rocket zooming across the field. But it gets even cooler when it comes to his decision-making. In those split seconds, Messi made high-pressure choices that most of us couldn't make in a calm Sunday game of backyard soccer. Each move was calculated, precise, and executed with the confidence of a seasoned pro.

Media and Fan Reaction

The reaction was wild! Fans went nuts, and the media were all over it, splashing headlines that screamed, "Messi emulates Maradona!" This goal didn't just light up the scoreboard; it lit up Messi's career. People started seeing him not just as a talented player of his time but as someone who could stand shoulder to shoulder with the legends of the game. It was the kind of goal that people rewind and watch over and over, each time feeling that rush of excitement as if it's happening live.

Career Trajectory Influence

So, what did this mean for young Messi? It gave him confidence, for starters. Scoring such a stunner in a high-stakes match pumped him up like nothing else. It also set the bar high, not just for him but for every other player out there. Messi was no longer just a part of the conversation about the world's best players; he was leading it. This goal was a turning point, propelling him into a career that would be marked by unbelievable goals, breathtaking games, and a legacy that kids and adults alike would admire for generations.

As we look back at this defining moment, it's clear why Messi's name is spoken with such reverence. It's not just about the goals; it's about the moments of pure brilliance that remind us why we love soccer so much. So, next time you see Messi dribble past defenders with ease, remember this match because it was the moment Messi stamped his name on the heart of soccer.

Ronaldo's Hat Trick for Portugal Against Spain in 2018 WC

The World Cup is the biggest stage in soccer, where legends are made and remembered. Added to that mix, in 2018, was a high-voltage clash between neighboring rivals Portugal and

Spain. The air was electric, the stakes were sky-high, and every player on the field knew that this wasn't just another game. Right in the heart of this drama stood none other than Cristiano Ronaldo, Portugal's captain and talisman. On this pulsating evening in Sochi, Ronaldo wasn't just playing in a crucial World Cup match; he was about to etch a tale of legendary proportions into the annals of fútbol history.

Ronaldo's performance in this match was a masterclass in soccer excellence. With the world watching, he stepped up and delivered three stunning goals, each marking a different aspect of his vast fútbol prowess. This wasn't just a display of skill; it was a statement of resilience and sheer willpower.

The match was a roller coaster of emotions, with Spain pulling ahead only for Ronaldo to bring Portugal back into the game each time. His last-minute free kick—a curling, gravity-defying shot that sailed into the top corner of the net—was the stuff of pure soccer magic. It tied the game at 3–3 and completed his hat trick, sending fans and commentators into a frenzy. It was a moment of pure theatrical brilliance, perfectly scripted and flawlessly executed.

But Ronaldo's goals were not merely a display of skill, they were a demonstration of his leadership that day. Being a captain is about more than wearing an armband; it's about stepping up when your team needs you the most, and boy, did Ronaldo step up! Each of his goals came at a moment when Portugal needed a morale boost, when the pressure was mounting and the odds were tilting in Spain's favor. His ability to seize these critical moments and turn them into opportunities is what makes him a true leader. It's one thing to perform when the going is easy, but to do so under intense pressure—to rally your team and carry them on your shoulders—that's what makes a legend.

Tactically, Ronaldo's role in this match was a brilliant showcase of adaptability and strategic thinking. Positioned primarily as a striker, he was constantly on the move, pulling Spanish defenders out of position and creating space for his teammates. His movements were purposeful and intelligent, designed to exploit the gaps in Spain's defense. Ronaldo's understanding of the game's flow and his ability to adapt to different situations were on full display. He was bending their opponents' formations and stretching their strategies at his will.

This match cemented Ronaldo's legacy as one of the greatest fútbol players of all time. Scoring a hat trick in such a high-stakes match against a top team like Spain is no small feat. It showed off Ronaldo's enduring quality and his ability to influence the biggest matches. His performance reminded everyone that, even in the twilight of his career, he could still dominate the world's biggest stage, delivering performances that resonated far beyond the final whistle. For Ronaldo, this game was a reaffirmation of his greatness—a loud and clear reminder of his ability to shape not just games but tournaments and legacies with his skill, determination, and sheer force of will.

Neymar's Performance Against PSG in the 2017 Champions League

Imagine being down 4–0 after the first leg of a Champions League knockout round; most teams and their players would throw in the towel, right? But not Barcelona, and certainly not Neymar. The stage was set at Camp Nou for one of the most thrilling comebacks in fútbol history, and Neymar was about to turn into the conductor of this symphony. The clock was ticking down, the odds were stacked high, and then, magic sparked. Neymar stepped up— a hero destined to etch this night into the eternal memories of fútbol fans around the world. In the dying minutes of the match, his contributions were nothing short of miraculous. Scoring two crucial goals and assisting the decisive sixth, Neymar transformed despair into joy, disbelief into awe, and a looming exit into a historic victory.

Neymar's mental fortitude during this match was the stuff of legends. His team needed three goals to advance, and the clock was not his friend. The weight of expectation was crushing, the stadium was a cauldron of nerves, and every touch of the ball was met with the collective heartbeat of tens of thousands of fans in the stands. In these moments, Neymar's composure was unshakeable.

His ability to perform under such immense pressure didn't just demonstrate his physical skill; it showcased a mental strength that defines great players. Each dribble, each pass, and each decision was made with a calmness that belied the chaos of the situation. Neymar was battling against the odds, driven by an inner belief that even the impossible is possible.

Now, let's talk about the sheer brilliance of his fútbol skills that night. Neymar's dribbling was a masterclass in agility and control; he maneuvered through PSG's defense with the elegance of a ballet dancer and the precision of a surgeon. His passes were strategic masterpieces, slicing through the opposition's setup with pinpoint accuracy. But the crown jewel of his performance was the free kick that reignited his team—an exquisite long-distance curler that whispered into the net as if guided by some otherworldly force. And when the pressure was sky-high, Neymar took the responsibility of a crucial penalty, slotting it home with a coolness that froze the Parisian spirits.

The aftermath of this epic showdown was profound, not just for Barcelona but also for Neymar himself. His dazzling performance caught the eyes of none other than PSG—the very club left devastated by his brilliance. They saw in Neymar not just a world-class talent but a game-changer—a player whose individual brilliance could turn the tides of the most dire matches.

The result was a record-breaking transfer fee that saw Neymar move to Paris Saint-Germain in a bid to bring his magic to the French capital. PSG believed in his ability to be not just a player but a creator of greatness—an investment in turning their own Champions League dreams into realities.

As we reflect on that unforgettable night, it becomes clear that this was more than just a match. Neymar's performance was a vivid reminder of why fútbol is so passionately followed around the globe. It's moments like these—where skill, determination, and heart converge on the grand stage— that lift fútbol from a mere sport to a compelling story filled with heroes and legends. And on that magical night at Camp Nou, Neymar walked into the records of fútbol history, leaving behind a legacy that would be talked about for generations to come.

Mbappé's World Cup Heroics for France

Hold onto your hats because we're about to zoom through one of the most electrifying chapters in World Cup history, starring none other than Kylian Mbappé. The year was 2018, and the soccer world was about to witness a teenager not only compete but *star* on the world's biggest stage. Mbappé wasn't just part of France's squad; he was a whirlwind of speed and skill that blew through defenses like a tornado through a cornfield. From his first game to lifting the trophy, Mbappé was nothing short of sensational, playing a pivotal role in game after game and proving that age is just a number when you're born to play soccer.

Now, let's rewind to a match that really put Mbappé on everyone's radar: the knockout game against Argentina. Here was this young guy, facing off against seasoned legends, and what did he do? He ran the show. Scoring twice and winning a penalty, he turned what was expected to be a tightly contested match into the Kylian Mbappé show. His performance demonstrated bursts of speed, sharp cuts, and cool finishes. Watching him play was phenomenal.

Comparing Mbappé to another soccer legend, Pelé, brings another layer of wow to his performances. Think about it: Pelé—one of the greatest ever—made his mark in the World Cup as a teenager, and here was Mbappé, doing the same. Both players not only played but excelled and left indelible marks on their tournaments. Mbappé's ability to shine so brightly at such a young age draws a direct line to Pelé, reminding everyone that great talent can emerge at any age. This demonstrates the impact and inspiration that these young players provide, showing that the torch of soccer greatness is always ready to be passed to the next generation.

Mbappé's speed and decision-making are worth their own highlight reel. Throughout the tournament, his ability to accelerate from 0 to 60 in the blink of an eye left both fans and defenders in awe. But speed without smarts is like a sports car without a steering wheel—it looks cool but isn't going to get you very far. Mbappé, however, knew exactly when to sprint, when to slow down, and when to make his move. His decision-making in split-second situations was impeccable. During the match against Argentina, each time Mbappé got the ball, you could feel the anticipation buzzing through the crowd because they knew he was about to do something amazing.

This incredible journey through the World Cup not only ended with a trophy, it also catapulted Mbappé into the stratosphere of soccer fame. Suddenly, he was a global superstar, his name known in every corner of the world. The expectations placed on his shoulders grew exponentially, but so did his influence. Young kids started looking up to him not just as a player but as a hero—an icon who had shown that with talent, determination, and a bit of fearlessness, the sky's the limit. His performances set the stage for a career that many are watching closely, eager to see just how high this star can soar.

Haaland's Champions League Record for Salzburg

Imagine stepping onto the Champions League stage for the first time. For most players, it's a nerve-wracking experience filled with what-ifs. But for Erling Haaland, it was like stepping into his backyard; he was ready to play, have fun, and oh, smash some records along the way! In his debut

Champions League season with RB Salzburg, Haaland was a goal-scoring machine set on turbo mode. From his very first game, he made the net dance, scoring a hat trick against Genk and announcing himself to the world, not with a whisper but with a roar that echoed across the soccer universe.

Now, let's break down exactly what made Haaland's goal-scoring spree in the Champions League so special: Each goal was a showcase of his incredible soccer smarts. His spatial awareness, for instance, was like having a built-in GPS that was always tuned to the goal. Whether it was finding the perfect spot in the box or positioning himself to receive a pass, Haaland always knew where to be at the right time. Then, there's his shooting accuracy; each shot was like a sniper's bullet, aimed with precision and lethal in execution. But what really set him apart was his physical prowess. Haaland combined the agility of a gymnast with the power of a sprinter, making him an unstoppable force in the penalty area.

But Haaland's impact wasn't just about the goals he scored; it was about how he transformed RB Salzburg's approach in the Champions League. His presence on the field meant that opponents couldn't rest easy for even a second. Defenders had to constantly track his movements, often pulling them out of position and creating opportunities for his teammates. This tactical advantage allowed Salzburg to play a more dynamic, aggressive game, challenging some of the best teams in Europe with confidence. Haaland was both a player *and* a strategy—a weapon that Salzburg wielded with precision and pride.

The ripples of Haaland's performances spread far beyond just Salzburg, however. His explosive entry into the

Champions League caught the eyes of top clubs across Europe. Scouts and managers scribbled notes furiously, all asking the same question: "How can we get Haaland on our team?" His market value skyrocketed, a meteoric rise that matched his on-field exploits. His performance ignited not only a transfer interest but also a race where the prize was this young striker who had proven himself capable of dazzling on the biggest stage in club fútbol. Haaland's early Champions League games set the stage for a high-profile move that would soon see him donning the colors of Borussia Dortmund.

As we wrap up this exciting section on Haaland's record-breaking debut in the Champions League, it's clear that his entry was not just memorable but historic. From his hat trick in his first game to becoming a key player for Salzburg, Haaland's journey in the tournament was a blitz of goals, records, and jaw-dropping moments. His impact on the team, their opponents, and the fútbol market showed that he was a player who was not just participating in the Champions League but redefining what a debutant could achieve.

What's next for Haaland? Only time will tell, but one thing is for sure: The world will be watching, eager for more of those moments that make us all jump from our seats and shout at the top of our lungs.

As we close this chapter, we're reminded that in fútbol, as in life, sometimes a fresh face and a fearless spirit can turn the game on its head, challenging the old guard and bringing a new thrill to the beautiful game. But regardless of age, we know that the most crucial key to success is a killer combination of mental resilience and physical skill. Onward to more adventures, more goals, and more record-smashing performances!

Chapter 4:

Challenges and Resilience

This chapter is like the epic boss level in your favorite video game, where our soccer heroes face their biggest challenges yet. But just like any game worth its salt, overcoming these tough spots is what makes victory feel oh-so-sweet.

Today, we're diving into the gritty, not-so-glamorous parts of being a soccer superstar. It's not all about dazzling goals and lifting trophies. Sometimes, it's about facing down the tough stuff and coming out stronger on the other side. So, let's lace up our boots and take a walk through the rocky roads these legends traveled. It's going to be a bumpy ride, but hey, that's where all the fun is, right?

Messi's Battle With Growth Hormone Deficiency

Diagnosis and Early Struggles

Imagine you're running around, scoring goals, and dreaming of playing soccer professionally someday, but then, *boom!* You find out you have a growth hormone deficiency that might put those dreams on hold. As we touched on in

Chapter 1, that's exactly what happened to Lionel Messi when he was 11. His doctors said he needed treatment to grow properly, which was not only super scary but also kind of a big deal for his future in soccer. Young Messi faced a mountain of uncertainty, with questions swirling around: Would he grow tall enough to compete? Could he still play the sport he loved? It was a tough time filled with lots of worries for little Lionel and his family.

Treatment and Sacrifices

Now, this treatment that Messi needed wasn't just a one-shot deal; it was expensive and had to be done regularly. His family wasn't made of money, and the cost was like a goalkeeper blocking their path. But when Messi was 13, things took a turn. FC Barcelona—yes, the big, famous soccer club—offered to help. They saw Messi's incredible talent and said, "Hey, we believe in this kid. Let's offer to pay for his treatment if he'll move to Spain and join our youth team." Imagine that! It was a huge relief but also a massive decision. Moving to a new country, leaving friends behind, and starting anew in a place where you don't even speak the language? That's what I call a major-league life change! But Messi, backed by his family's support, decided to take the leap (or kick, if you will).

Overcoming the Odds

Fast forward through all the treatments, the homesickness, and the new challenges in a different land. Not only did Messi keep growing, but his soccer skills exploded like a firework! He zipped past defenders, scored crazy goals, and basically played like he was in a video game set on easy mode. All those treatments—along with the move and adjustments—paid off big time. Messi didn't just overcome his health challenge; he smashed it into the back of the net. He showed all those folks who doubted him that yes, he was short, but no, that wasn't going to stop him from becoming one of the greatest soccer players the world has ever seen.

Psychological Impact

Let's talk about the mind game here: Dealing with a growth hormone deficiency wasn't just a physical challenge for Messi; it was a mental marathon too. From a young age, he had to cope with big worries and pressures that most kids never even have to think about. But he handled it like a champ. He developed an incredible mental toughness—a sort of superpower that let him stay focused, keep pushing, and never stop dreaming, no matter how tough things got. This resilience became one of his secret weapons, allowing him to face any challenge, on or off the field, with a cool head and a steady heart.

So, as we wrap up Messi's part of our rocky road tour, remember that even the greatest heroes have their hurdles. But it's not just about jumping over them; it's about what you learn on the way down. Messi's story isn't just a tale of soccer success; it's also a lesson in never giving up, no matter what life throws at you. Whether it's a weird bounce of the ball or a health hiccup, the game isn't over until the final whistle blows. Keep playing, keep dreaming, and who knows? The next chapter of your story might just be the best one yet.

Ronaldo's Recovery From His 2008 Knee Injury

Imagine you're Cristiano Ronaldo: fast, flashy, and at the top of your game. Then, during a match in 2008, your world comes crashing down, not from a tackle or a bad fall but from your knee suddenly deciding, "Nope, I'm done here." That's right, Ronaldo faced a gnarly knee injury. Specifically, his right knee had a torn patellar tendon—the fiber that attaches the thigh muscle to the kneecap, allowing a person to run and kick. Ouch! Talk about bad timing, right?

This wasn't just a small hiccup; it was the kind of injury that could have put a stop to his blazing career. The fears started pouring in: Would he ever sprint again? Could he return to his best? The whispers of doubt were as loud as a stadium crowd, but Ronaldo was not about to let this injury bench him for good.

Now, onto the gritty part: rehabilitation. Ronaldo's recovery was a monumental task. While everyone else was playing and training on the field, Ronaldo was in the gym, pushing his healing body to restore itself. His rehab process involved everything from basic knee exercises to advanced strength and conditioning drills. The goal? To get that knee back in action and stronger than ever.

This wasn't just a physical battle; it was a full-on war against his own limits. With each stretch, each lift, and each step, Ronaldo was fighting to reclaim his place on the field. His dedication was fierce. Mornings, afternoons, and evenings, you'd find him sweating it out, determined to come back stronger. This level of commitment was inspirational, showcasing his relentless drive and unyielding determination to return to peak form.

Fast forward a bit, and the moment of truth arrives: Ronaldo's return to the pitch. The buzz was electric. Fans, teammates, and even rivals waited with bated breath to see if the star had dimmed or if he was still the fútbol wizard they knew. Spoiler alert: Ronaldo was not just back; he was back with a bang! From his very first game post-injury, he was a whirlwind on the field, sprinting, scoring, and showing off that trademark Ronaldo flair.

But there was a slight twist in his style. Post-injury, Ronaldo tweaked his gameplay. He became more strategic, relying less on sheer speed and more on sharpshooting and cunning moves. This slight shift made him not just a fast player but a smart one too. His ability to adapt and adjust his style post-recovery not only kept him in top form but also added a new layer to his game, making him unpredictable and even more challenging for defenders.

Throughout this ordeal, Ronaldo's mental game was as tough as his physical recovery. Injuries can mess with your head, filling it with doubts and what-ifs. But Ronaldo used this setback as fuel, turning each pang of frustration into a stepping stone toward greatness.

His mental strength during this period was a masterclass in sports psychology. He embraced the challenge and used the injury as motivation to not only return but to go above and beyond. This mindset—this refusal to be beaten by circumstance—kept him pushing through the pain, the rehab, and the long hours. It's what solidified his legacy as a true legend of the game. His resilience and perseverance serve as a blueprint for any athlete facing the daunting road of recovery.

So, as Ronaldo laced his boots and stepped onto the pitch, each game spoke to the power of his incredible journey back from what could have been a career-ending injury. His comeback story is a vivid reminder that true champions aren't just born; they're forged through trials, pain, and an unbreakable will to overcome. Ronaldo's journey through injury, recovery, and triumph is a powerful chapter in the epic saga of his career, reminding us all that no obstacle is too big when you have the heart of a champion.

Neymar's Back Injury in the 2014 World Cup

The 2014 World Cup was a super-hyped global event, especially since it was happening right in Brazil, Neymar's home turf. Picture this: The crowd's roaring, the stakes are high, and Neymar is zipping across the field like a superhero. But then, blink-and-you'll-miss-it fast, during the quarter-final against Colombia, everything takes a dramatic turn. Neymar goes down, and it's not just a simple trip or slip. He's in serious pain. A knee to his back during a challenge has left him sprawled on the ground, and just like that, Brazil's golden boy is out of the tournament. The stadium goes from loud cheers to a hushed silence, the kind that screams, "Oh no! This can't be happening!"

The aftermath was like a drama series finale. Neymar was rushed off with a fractured vertebra, and the news hit fans like a punch to the gut. Back home, people were glued to their TVs, waiting for updates, while the global media buzzed with speculation and concern. Could Brazil continue their World Cup dream without their star player? The mood was tense, a cocktail of worry and hope, because let's face it, Neymar wasn't just any player; he was, and still is, a beacon of samba soccer magic.

Now, let's talk about the ripple effects of that one incident: With Neymar sidelined, Brazil's squad felt the pinch. In the very next game, they faced Germany, and oh boy, it wasn't pretty. Brazil's World Cup hopes were crushed under a brutal 7–1 loss. It was clear as day; Neymar's absence left a hole in the team's spirit and strategy that just couldn't be patched up in time. But it wasn't just a short-term bummer; for Neymar, this injury was a major pause button on his rocketing career. Questions popped up like popcorn: Would he bounce back? Could he still be the same electrifying player post-recovery? It was a cliffhanger that had everyone biting their nails.

Cut to the recovery phase: Neymar's journey back to the pitch was no walk in the park. He had to go through weeks of rehab, physiotherapy sessions that probably felt longer than a bad movie, and a cocktail of recovery routines. But here's where Neymar's true colors shone through: Instead of letting the injury keep him down, he tackled his recovery with the same zest he shows on the field. Each session was a step toward getting back his groove, and you bet he worked as hard off the field as he did on it.

Neymar's comeback was emotional, not just for him but for his fans too. When he finally laced up his boots and hit the grass again, it wasn't just a return; it was a rebirth. The crowd went wild, the cheers were back, and Neymar was smiling, playing, and yes, scoring.

This whole ordeal, as tough as it was, added a new layer to Neymar's persona, both on and off the field. He was no longer solely known for his flashy footwork or goals. Now, public respect for Neymar was about his resilience—the kind that toughens you up and polishes your spirit.

Neymar emerged not only recovered but also evolved. His game matured, showing more grit and a deeper understanding of what it means to fight back. It was like watching your favorite superhero get knocked down, only to come back stronger, wiser, and ready to dazzle again. Neymar's comeback story is evidence of his fighting spirit, reminding us all that, sometimes, the toughest challenges forge the greatest legends. And as he once again danced past defenders and charmed the crowds, it was clear that Neymar was back to wow, to inspire, and to continue weaving his magic on the soccer world stage.

Mbappé's Struggles With Early Fame and Expectations

Imagine that you're a normal teenager, and suddenly, you're not just kicking the ball at the local park with your friends; you're scoring goals in the world's biggest stadiums, with millions watching, cheering, and expecting you to be the next big thing every single game. That's exactly what happened to Kylian Mbappé. His rise to stardom was like a rocket launch. One day, he was a talented young player, and the next, he was being hailed as the future of soccer. Talk about pressure, right? Everyone expecting you to win, all the time, cannot be an easy thing to deal with!

Handling this kind of fame is like juggling soccer balls while riding a unicycle. After his standout performances in the World Cup—where he wasn't just good but spectacular— Mbappé found himself under the intense glare of the media spotlight. His every move, both on and off the field, was scrutinized. Did he score? Did he assist? Did he smile at the camera right? It was relentless.

For many, this kind of attention could be overwhelming, but Mbappé managed it with a maturity that's rare. He understood that his performances set a standard, and with each game, he was not just playing for fun but carrying the hopes of millions. This meant dealing with reporters' microphones being shoved in his face after every match, experts dissecting his every move, and the constant buzz of social media chatter about every aspect of his life.

Balancing all this fame with a personal life was a whole new level of challenge. Imagine trying to have a normal day out with friends or family, and there are cameras following you, fans asking for autographs, and always, always the expectation to be "Mbappé the Star," even when you're just trying to be Kylian, the guy who loves a good laugh and some video games.

For Mbappé, keeping his personal life balanced with his professional life became a crucial skill. He had to learn how to switch off the "star mode" and just be a young guy enjoying life. This wasn't easy, especially with his skyrocketing fame, but it was essential for keeping his sanity in the mad world of international soccer.

Mentally, dealing with this new life required a ton of growth from Mbappé. He had to mature faster than most people his age, handling both the physical demands of the game and the mental and emotional roller coasters that come with being thrust into the limelight.

Imagine having millions of eyes on you, expecting you to be perfect, to never falter, and to always be the hero. That's a heavy load. But Mbappé—with the support of family, coaches, and teammates—managed to navigate these waters with remarkable grace. He learned to embrace the expectations and see them not as burdens but as challenges to rise above. He developed a mental toughness—a shield that helped him keep his focus on the field and his joy of the game intact, despite the swirling vortex of fame and pressure around him.

Kylian Mbappé's story tells vividly of a rapid rise, immense pressure, and the quest for balance. It's about a young soccer phenomenon handling the whirlwind of early fame with a composure that's as impressive as his lightning speed on the pitch.

Watching him play, you can see more than just his goals and victories; you see a young man who's growing, learning, and embracing his part as a role model for millions. His journey has been filled with challenges but also with incredible moments of triumph, both on and off the field. As he continues to dazzle us with his skills, Mbappé not only scores goals but also wins hearts, showing us all how to handle the spotlight with a smile and a step-over.

Haaland's Adaptation to Different Leagues and Injury Setbacks

Have you ever thought, *Woah, this is tough*, after moving to a new school or jumping into a new game level? Well, imagine how intense that feeling must be when you step into the world of professional soccer across many different countries. That's a slice of Erling Haaland's life. Starting in Norway, moving to Austria, and then charging into Germany, each league was a new adventure—a fresh challenge waiting to test his skills and adaptability.

When Haaland kicked off his career in Norway with Bryne, and then moved to Molde, he was already turning heads. But moving to RB Salzburg in Austria was his first major leap into a bigger pond. He needed to learn how to handle meeting new teammates, learning a different playing style, and oh, the pressure of having to prove himself all over again. But Haaland didn't just fit in; he shone like a bright star on a clear night. His time in Austria was like a turbo boost, propelling his career forward at rocket speed.

However, the real test came when he signed with Borussia Dortmund in Germany—a top-tier team known for its fierce competition. The Bundesliga was a whole new ball game, but Haaland laced up, ready to sprint. Adapting to this level meant understanding faster gameplay, tougher opponents, and more complex tactics. Yet, Haaland knew that every match was a chance for him to learn, adjust, and showcase that, yes, he could dance this new, intense soccer tango.

Like any top athlete, Haaland has had his share of injury timeouts—knee problems, muscle issues, you name it. Each injury was a hurdle—a pause in his sprint up the soccer ladder. But his approach to recovery has been nothing short of inspirational. Haaland treats each setback like a puzzle to solve.

With a team of doctors, physios, and coaches, along with his own iron will, he focuses on coming back stronger. Recovery for Haaland is never just about healing; it's about refining his body, understanding its limits, and strengthening it to prevent future injuries. This proactive approach turns potential setbacks into strategic pit stops, giving him the resilience to bounce back game after game.

When it comes to consistency, Haaland's middle name should be "Mr. Reliable." Despite the league changes and injuries, his performance has remained top-notch. Scoring goals, setting up plays, and being a team player, he's kept his standards sky-high.

This consistency is true of both his approach to physical fitness and his determination to build mental toughness. Imagine the focus it takes to perform at your best, game after game, no matter the league or the country. Haaland's ability to maintain such high standards across different teams and conditions shows an emotional intelligence in his gameplay and an adaptability that's rare and remarkable. It's like he has a soccer GPS that recalibrates and ensures he's always on the right track, no matter where he's playing.

Through all the league transitions and injury challenges, Haaland has truly evolved as a player. Each new league has added layers to his game—be it faster decision-making, better spatial awareness, or sharper shooting. It's like each season unleashes a new version of Haaland, upgraded and updated. This cycle of continuous learning and evolution makes him not just a player to watch but a player to study. How does he adapt so quickly? What keeps him so consistent? The answers lie in his relentless pursuit of improvement, his resilience against setbacks, and his sheer love for the game.

As this chapter closes, remember that every new challenge is a chance to get better. Haaland's journey through different leagues and overcoming injuries is more than just a sports story; it's a playbook for facing life's tough matches with determination and a never-quit attitude. Whether you're a budding soccer player or just a fan, there's a lesson in the stories of the greats for everyone. Keep playing, keep learning, and who knows? The next chapter might just be your best one yet.

So, as we step into the next part of this book, let's carry forward this spirit of resilience and adaptability. After all, isn't that what makes fútbol so incredibly awesome? It teaches us to keep pushing, keep evolving, and most importantly, to never stop playing the game, no matter what challenges come our way. Let's keep the ball rolling!

Chapter 5:

Peak Performances

This chapter is about how our favorite players have blasted expectations out of the park and set records that make even the stat books sweat! As usual, we're kicking off with none other than Lionel Messi. In 2012, this soccer wizard did something so wild, so out there, it was like someone had handed him a cheat code. Ready to dive into the year Messi decided to rewrite history? Let's get the ball rolling!

Messi's Record-Breaking 91 Goals in 2012

Historical Context

Let's set the scene: The year is 2012. The world didn't end like the Mayans predicted, but in the world of soccer, a bombshell was about to drop. The air in stadiums was thick with anticipation as teams across the globe were gunning for glory. But amidst the fierce competition and soccer cleats clashing, one little magician from Argentina was about to pull a rabbit out of his hat—or rather, 91 rabbits out of 91 different hats. The stage was set, and Messi was ready to not just play the game but change it forever.

Game-by-Game Breakdown

Imagine a highlight reel so long, you'd need to grab popcorn thrice while watching it. That was Messi in 2011–12. Game after game, this guy was on fire, blazing trails on the field. Whether it was a nutmeg here, a dribble there, or a free kick that made the crowd go wild, Messi was unstoppable. But it wasn't just about scoring goals; it was about when and how he scored them. Clutch moments? Check. Big games? Check. Left foot, right foot, header—you name it, he scored it. His hat trick against Malaga was epic. His double whammy against Real Madrid was jaw-dropping. Every match was a chance for Messi to show the world that records were meant to be broken.

Tactical Evolution

During 2012, Barcelona was like a well-oiled machine, and Messi was its most lethal component. Under managers like Pep Guardiola and, later, Tito Vilanova, Barca's style evolved into something that felt almost futuristic. Passes were so sharp, you'd think the ball was on a string.

Messi was often at the heart of it all, weaving through defenses with the ease of a hot knife through butter. But here's the kicker: Messi wasn't just a finisher; his role involved dropping deeper, linking up plays, and essentially acting as a "false 9"—a deeper-lying striker. This tactical tweak not only confused opponents but also allowed Messi to maximize his impact, turning him into a playmaker as well as a prolific scorer.

Legacy and Records

Breaking Gerd Müller's record of 85 goals in a calendar year, Messi set a new world record with 91 goals. His 2012 rampage wasn't just a personal triumph; it sent ripples across the soccer world. Suddenly, kids everywhere were trying to mimic his style, and they were dreaming bigger, pushing harder, and believing that maybe, just maybe, they could be like Messi too. His legacy was no longer just about the number of trophies or the dazzle of his play; it was about showing that limits exist to be pushed, boundaries to be crossed, and records to be shattered.

Messi's 2012 was a meteor shower of moments that soccer fans will talk about for generations. From his magical runs to his eye-popping goals, every touch of the ball was a brushstroke on the canvas of his ever-growing legend. As we move from one tale of soccer brilliance to another, remember that each game is not only 90 minutes on the clock but also a chance to create magic, just like Messi did.

Ronaldo's Triple Consecutive Ballon d'Or Wins

Alright, let's switch gears and discuss one of the coolest soccer-award feats. Yep, you guessed it; we're talking about Cristiano Ronaldo and his jaw-dropping hat trick of Ballon d'Or wins in 2013, 2014, and 2015. Winning the Ballon d'Or—the golden ticket of soccer accolades—just once is a huge deal. But snagging it three times in a row? That's like winning a video game on the hardest difficulty without losing a life!

Each of these years, Ronaldo was redefining what it meant to be a forward. His blend of speed, skill, and sheer determination made him a nightmare for defenders and a hero for fans. In critical Champions League clashes and explosive performances in major derbies, Ronaldo wasn't just participating; he was dominating. Each goal and each game was a step toward etching his name into the history books. For instance, when he scored a hat trick against Sweden in the World Cup playoffs, Ronaldo was not only securing Portugal's spot in the tournament but also staking his claim as the world's best.

But Ronaldo's magic wasn't just about what he did with the ball; it was about how he did it and whom he was up against. During these golden years, he faced some serious soccer royalty: names like Lionel Messi—who could dribble through defenses like they were traffic cones—and Manuel Neuer, a goalkeeper so good he could probably stop a meteor from hitting the earth. Yet, Ronaldo managed to shine the brightest. His stats were off the charts—goals, assists, you name it. It was his ability to perform consistently at this sky-high level that set him apart. Not just any player can turn it up a notch on the biggest stages against the toughest opponents, but Ronaldo did just that, again and again.

Now, let's talk about the ripple effects of these wins, both for Ronaldo and Real Madrid. Each golden trophy boosted Ronaldo's personal cabinet, which mirrored Real Madrid's rise and dominance in European soccer. The club's success in the Champions League—including "La Decima," their tenth title—wasn't just about good team dynamics; it was propelled by Ronaldo's goals and leadership.

Off the field, these victories catapulted him into his status as a global icon—a brand as much as a player—influencing everything from jersey sales to social media followers. His marketability soared to new heights, making him a household name across the globe.

Ronaldo's trio of Ballon d'Or wins were celebrations of his relentless ambition, his incredible skill, and the never-say-die attitude that transformed every game he played. Through these awards, Ronaldo not only claimed the title of the world's best player, but he also inspired millions, showing that with hard work and passion, taking the soccer world by the storm isn't just a dream but a very achievable reality. As he lifted each Ballon d'Or trophy, it was a reminder to all of us that greatness awaits those who are willing to chase it down with every ounce of their being.

Neymar's Strategic Mastery in the 2015 Treble Season

Have you ever watched a magician pull off a trick so smoothly that you just sat there wondering if magic might actually be real? That's what watching Neymar during Barcelona's treble-winning 2014–15 season was like. It seemed as though this guy wasn't just playing soccer; he was weaving spells on the field, making the ball disappear from right under defenders' noses and reappear in the back of the net. That season, Neymar turned soccer into a fine art, with every dribble, pass, and goal a stroke of genius.

In 2014–15, Barcelona not only clinched the La Liga title but also bagged the Copa del Rey and the UEFA Champions League. Yep, they grabbed the big three, and Neymar was front and center in this fútbol fiesta. His impact was undeniable.

In La Liga, his moves were so slick that defenders probably got whiplash trying to keep up. His ability to sync with teammates and anticipate their movements made every match feel like a well-rehearsed dance routine, with the other team missing all their steps. And in the Copa del Rey, Neymar turned it up a notch, transforming games into his personal highlight reels. But the real cherry on top was the Champions League, where his flair for dramatic goals helped Barcelona outshine Europe's best, proving that when it came to big games, Neymar was taking over.

But let's dive deeper into the tactics because, oh wow, was it a masterclass! Barcelona's coach at the time knew exactly how to maximize Neymar's skills. Neymar, Messi, and Suarez—three of soccer's biggest names—were all in one team. It sounds like a dream, right? Well, this dream became the best possible reality.

Neymar's role often saw him drifting from the left flank towards the center, creating a fluid attacking trio that defenders found impossible to pin down. This was by design. Barcelona's tactical flexibility allowed Neymar to roam, drift, and dart exactly where he was needed, making the team's attack not just dynamic but downright unpredictable. Whether he was slicing through defenses like a hot knife through butter or pulling off one-twos with Messi or Suarez, Neymar's adaptability on the field was a key ingredient in Barcelona's recipe for success.

In the Champions League knockout stages, each game was a high-stakes drama, and Neymar was always ready for his close-up. Against PSG in the quarter-finals, his goals were like exclamation points, punctuating a performance that screamed top-class. And in the final against Juventus, Neyman's goal wasn't just the icing on the cake but also the sparkler on top, sealing the deal and the treble for Barcelona. In these games, Neymar proved time and again that pressure wasn't something to buckle under but, rather, something to rise above.

But here's the kicker: Neymar's influence went beyond just scoring goals; he was also making everyone around him better. His ability to draw defenders opened up spaces wider than a highway, giving his teammates room to maneuver and strike. His vision for spotting a pass meant he could thread the ball through the eye of a needle, setting up goals that sometimes looked like they defied physics. This knack for creating opportunities made Neymar a triple threat—scorer, playmaker, and team player, all rolled into one. His contributions that season showed that soccer isn't just about how many goals you score but also how you play the game, elevate your team, and leave a mark on every match.

As we look back on that magical season, it's clear Neymar wasn't just part of Barcelona's success; he was a driving force behind it. With every dribble, goal, and jaw-dropping play, he helped write a chapter of soccer history that fans will talk about for years to come. Whether you're a die-hard Barcelona fan or just a lover of beautiful soccer, Neyman's performance during the 2014–15 season was a reminder of why we watch sports in the first place—for the moments of unexpected brilliance that make us believe in magic, even if it's just on the soccer field.

Mbappé's Acceleration to PSG's Leading Scorer

In 2017, Kylian Mbappé was a teenager who had just swapped Monaco's red and white for PSG's iconic blue, joining one of the world's most glamorous soccer clubs. From the get-go, Mbappé wasn't just part of Paris Saint-Germain; he was setting it on fire with his speed, skill, and hunger for goals—a desire that would see him shatter records time and time again.

Mbappé's arrival at PSG was like flipping the switch on a turbocharged engine. The team was already stacked with stars, but Mbappé brought something special: a blistering pace and an eye for goals that turned games into spectacles. His first season was spectacular. Match after match, he dazzled fans by tearing defenses apart and scoring goals that had a touch of everything—speed, precision, and flair. But it wasn't just the how of his goals that amazed people; it was the when. Clutch moments seemed to be his thing. Need a last-minute winner? Call on Mbappé. A big game where the stakes are sky-high? Oh, Mbappé's got this. His knack for being in the right place at the right time was uncanny, almost like he had a script of the game etched in his mind.

Diving deeper into his most explosive season, let's zoom in on 2018–19: With 33 goals, Mbappé clinched the Ligue 1 top-scorer award at just 20 years old. Each goal was evidence of his evolution from a speedy winger to a lethal striker. Long-range rockets, cheeky chips, and bullet headers: His arsenal was as varied as it was effective. And how he scored just kept impressive audiences and professionals alike. In a game against Lyon, with only the keeper to beat, Mbappé performed a stutter step so cool that it froze the keeper in place, allowing him to slot the ball home with a grin. It was these moments that made many of us realize that we were witnessing the growth of a soccer phenomenon.

Mbappé's impact on PSG's tactics was profound. The coach—whether it was Unai Emery or Thomas Tuchel—knew they had a gem, and they polished it well. Mbappé was often deployed not just as a winger but as a central striker, a role that allowed him to use his speed directly against the heart of the opponent's defense.

This tactical tweak was crucial. It gave PSG a sharper edge, turning their attack from dangerous to downright terrifying. Mbappé's ability to pull defenders out of position created oceans of space for his teammates, making the entire team more effective. As a result, PSG's gameplay evolved into a more dynamic, more aggressive style, all orchestrated to maximize Mbappé's impact. Whether it was in domestic leagues or the glittering stages of the Champions League, Mbappé's presence was a game-changer, literally and tactically.

Recognition and awards naturally followed. The accolades poured in, each one a shiny testament to his prowess. Being named Ligue 1 Player of the Year was a nod to his influence on the team and the league. Young Player awards seemed to be tailor-made for him, acknowledging not only his skill but also his ability to inspire a new generation of fútbol players. Every trophy and every accolade added to his growing legacy, marking him as not just a star player but also as a beacon for young talents everywhere.

As Mbappé continues to dazzle at PSG—and Real Madrid from July 1st, 2024—each game will be a chance to see a master at work and a young legend in the making. His journey has involved a blend of speed and skill, along with a relentless pursuit of greatness—a saga of a young star who took Paris by storm and made the fútbol world sit up and take notice. So, keep an eye on Mbappé. Whether he's sprinting down the field, setting up a teammate, or curling a ball into the net, you're not just watching fútbol; you're watching history in the making.

Haaland's Impact at Dortmund and Goal-Scoring Spree

Explosive Start

Imagine this: A young soccer player named Erling Haaland steps onto the pitch wearing the Borussia Dortmund jersey for the first time. It's like he's got rockets on his boots because, in this debut, he explodes onto the scene with a hat trick that leaves everyone's jaws on the floor. This isn't just any introduction; it's a blockbuster premiere in the soccer world. Picture the crowd, the noise, and this newcomer rewriting the script from the get-go.

Scoring three goals in his first match against Augsburg, Haaland didn't knock on the door of the Bundesliga; he kicked it down, announcing his arrival with the subtlety of a thunderclap. This stunning debut set the tone for what was to become a series of show-stopping performances, making it clear that Haaland wasn't just part of Dortmund's strategy; he was a headline act.

Record-Setting Performances

But Haaland didn't stop there. Oh no, he was just getting started. In his first Bundesliga season, he kept smashing records like they were piñatas at a birthday bash. He became the fastest person to reach 10 goals in Bundesliga history, as well as the youngest player to score 10 goals in a Champions League campaign.

Each game seemed like a chance for Haaland to etch his name deeper into the record books. His knack for being in the right place at the right time was uncanny. It was almost as if he could look a few seconds into the future of the game. Watching Haaland play during these record-setting months was like watching a highlight reel in real time. Each match added a new chapter to his rapidly growing legend, with fans and commentators alike running out of ways to describe his mind-blowing impact on the field.

Physical and Technical Attributes

Now, let's break down what makes Haaland such a formidable force on the pitch: First up is his speed. Haaland isn't just fast; he's a blur. This guy can sprint like he's got jet engines for legs, making it a nightmare for defenders trying to catch him. Then, there's his strength. Haaland has the physicality of a superhero, able to shrug off defenders as if they're little more than annoying flies buzzing around him. But what truly sets him apart is his clinical finishing. Give Haaland a sliver of space in front of the goal, and he'll punish you. He's not just shooting; he's calculating each shot with the precision of a master mathematician, finding angles that seem impossible and executing them with chilling efficiency.

Effect on Dortmund's Strategy

Haaland's arrival at Dortmund was like an energy shot to their tactical setup. Suddenly, Dortmund had a striker who could not only hold up play but also turn and sprint toward goal in seconds, disrupting any defensive plans the opposition might have had. His ability to draw multiple defenders created space for his teammates, which enhanced the team's overall dynamics.

With Haaland leading the line, Dortmund adopted a more direct approach, utilizing his speed and precision to devastating effect. This shift not only made the team more dangerous in attack but also more unpredictable, as opponents struggled to guess whether they'd play through the midfield or launch quick counters to exploit Haaland's explosive runs.

From his debut hat trick to shattering records and reshaping Dortmund's tactics, Haaland has not just lived up to the hype; he's blown it out of the water. Watching him play is like being in the front row of a blockbuster action movie, where every moment is edge-of-your-seat thrilling. And as we close this section, one thing is for sure: The Haaland show is just getting started. The soccer world can't wait to see what he does next.

In wrapping up, we can see how much our heroes' successes have been the outcomes of epic journeys of growth and change—both for them as individuals and for their teams, which needed to adapt to strategically make the most of their spectacular talents. This teaches us that our communities are some of our most important resources, and in the next chapter, we'll look at how these soccer greats used self-growth and positive leadership to go from strength to strength.

Chapter 6:

Leadership and Influence

Hey there, young soccer fan! Are you ready to dive into the world of soccer leadership? Well, you're in for a treat because we're about to explore how some of the biggest names in soccer are also captains of their teams in more ways than one. These soccer stars are like superheroes, but instead of fighting villains, they're leading their teams to victory and making a huge difference off the field too!

Messi's Leadership Style and His Youth Foundation Work

Evolution Into a Captain

Lionel Messi is a name that echoes in stadiums worldwide. But did you know he wasn't always the captain material we know today? Yep, Messi started as a shy kid who let his magical feet do the talking. But as he grew, both in age and skill, something cool happened: He evolved into a leader, not just for Barcelona but also for Argentina. Pretty awesome, right?

Now, Messi's style of leading is kind of like being the cool big brother. He's not the loudest in the room; instead, he leads by example. Imagine you're in a tough soccer match, the score is tied, and the pressure's mounting. Then, you see Messi calmly dribble through defenders and score a goal. Inspiring, isn't it? That's Messi for you. He shows everyone else how it's done, all while keeping cool under pressure—a trait that makes him a natural leader on the pitch.

Impact on Team Morale and Performance

Messi's calm demeanor has a super awesome effect on his team. When the going gets tough, the team looks at him and thinks, *If Messi isn't worried, why should we be?* This calmness spreads like a superpower, boosting team morale and performance, especially during nail-biting matches and tournaments. It's like he has a secret weapon that keeps everyone focused and driven, no matter how high the stakes are.

Philanthropic Initiatives

Off the field, Messi transforms into a superhero for kids all around the world through the Leo Messi Foundation. Launched in 2007, this foundation is all about helping kids with health care and education. Messi's not just scoring goals but also helping kids go to school and get better when they're sick. It's pretty much like he's scoring goals for humanity as a whole!

Mentorship Roles

But wait, there's more! Messi also plays a big role in mentoring younger players. Picture this: You're a new kid on the team, and Messi, yes, *the* Lionel Messi, comes over to give you tips. That's daily life for young players at Barcelona. Messi takes them under his wing, shares his experiences, and helps them navigate the pressures of professional soccer. They get to have their own personal soccer superstar by their side, offering guidance and support! How awesome is that?

Visual Element: Messi's Mentorship Tree

Exploring Messi's Impact

To give you a clearer picture of Messi's impact as a mentor, imagine a family tree, but instead of being chock-full of relatives, it's filled with young players who've grown under Messi's guidance. Each branch represents a player who's learned from the best, and each leaf is a person who has been impacted by or learned from these young players. This shows how Messi's mentorship helps new talents flourish, visually demonstrating how his influence extends far beyond his own career, nurturing the next generation of soccer stars.

So, as we've seen, being a leader in soccer isn't just about wearing the captain's armband; it's about setting positive examples, keeping cool under pressure, lifting team spirits, and giving back to the community. Messi does all this and more, proving that true leadership takes action both on and off the field.

Whether he's guiding young players or helping kids through his foundation, Messi knows that being a captain is about much more than just leading a team to victory. So, aim to make a positive impact in every way possible, and who knows? Maybe one day, you'll be the one young players look up to, both on and off the field! Keep playing, keep dreaming, and remember that the guidance of a true leader makes all the difference.

Ronaldo's Captaincy for Portugal and Charitable Contributions

Have you ever watched Cristiano Ronaldo on the field, charging forward, a blur of speed and skill, with a captain's armband snug on his arm? He's not just a player but a leader as well. His leadership style is loud, it's proud, and it's incredibly effective. Imagine being on the field and hearing Ronaldo's booming voice encouraging you, pushing you to dig deeper and play harder. That's what it's like for the Portuguese national team.

Moreover, Ronaldo's leadership is about how he lifts everyone around him. His speeches are full of passion and fire, and they can turn many people's doubt into determination, transforming the locker room atmosphere from nervous to charged-up in seconds.

Now, picture this: It's the Euro 2016 final, and disaster strikes. Ronaldo gets injured. You'd think that'd be it, right? Game over for the captain. But no, Ronaldo turned into Coach Ronaldo. Hobbling around on the sidelines, he shouted instructions and cheered like the world's most animated fan, becoming the ultimate motivator. Even from the sidelines, he's a leader, showing that a captain's influence isn't just about playing; it's about presence. He turned pain into inspiration, showing his team that even on one of the toughest nights of his career, he'd be there, fighting alongside them. That's leadership that you can't help but follow.

Switching gears from the field to the world at large, Ronaldo's heart is as big as his talent. His charitable work shows his commitment to giving back. Hospitals, children's charities, disaster relief efforts: You name it, Ronaldo's probably helped fund it. One of his notable acts is donating a whopping €1.5 million to feed people in Gaza. And let's not forget the time he paid for a 10-month-old baby's life-saving surgery.

These acts of kindness show a side of Ronaldo that goes beyond soccer. He uses his fame, his resources, and his time to make a difference and lift up those in need. Imagine being a kid in a hospital, and suddenly, Cristiano Ronaldo pops in to say hi and drop off a hefty donation for medical equipment. That's more than simple generosity; he's changing lives with the same passion he uses to change the outcomes of fútbol matches.

Ronaldo's influence stretches across the globe, touching fans and non-fans alike. His leadership and charitable actions speak a universal language of perseverance and compassion. Acting as more than a soccer player, he's a global ambassador of the sport, representing the importance of values like hard work and giving back. This global presence has made him a role model—an influencer in the truest sense of the word. Through his actions, both on and off the field, Ronaldo promotes a culture of hard work and helping others, inspiring millions to strive for greatness and think of others.

As you can see, being a captain is about much more than leading a team to victory. It's about inspiring those around you to be better, push harder, and remember that success isn't just about what you achieve for yourself but also about how you help others. Ronaldo embodies this spirit, showing that true greatness comes from the ability to lead and give back with equal passion.

Whether he's scoring goals, coaching from the sidelines, or helping children in need, Ronaldo lives up to the title of captain, not just for Portugal but for the world. So, next time you see him with that captain's armband, remember that it's not just a piece of fabric; it's a symbol of his commitment to lead, inspire, and support, both on and off the pitch.

Neymar's Influence at PSG and Involvement in Charity

When Neymar joined Paris Saint-Germain, he didn't just bring his dazzling dribbles and jaw-dropping goals; he also brought a whole new vibe to the team. Yep, Neymar's arrival at PSG was like a splash of colorful paint on a blank canvas. He wasn't just a player; he was a trendsetter, both on and off the field. His influence stretched far beyond scoring goals, seeping into how PSG players played, interacted, and even celebrated.

From day one, Neymar took on a role that was part cheerleader, part big brother, and all about making the team feel like a family. He was instrumental in helping new players settle in, showing them the ropes, and making sure they felt part of the PSG magic. His approach was all about creating a supportive environment where everyone could thrive. Neymar loved making friends, but he was also determined that PSG should be striving to build a team that played for each other, and he put himself at the heart of this transformation.

On the pitch, seeing Neymar's impact was like watching a master conductor lead an orchestra. Each pass and each move was part of a bigger strategy. He helped shape PSG's playing style to be more dynamic, more aggressive, and a lot more fun. If soccer was a dance, Neymar would've been the choreographer, introducing some sizzling new moves to PSG's repertoire.

The team's strategy evolved to make use of his strengths and get the most out of his speed and creativity. This shift not only made PSG tougher opponents but also made them more exciting to watch. Fans weren't just waiting for goals; they were eager to see what Neymar would do next, whether it was a slick pass, a solo run, or a combination play that left opponents dizzy.

Now, let's shift gears and talk about Neymar's magic off the field: his charitable work. Neymar isn't just about dazzling fans; he's deeply committed to using his fame for good. Take the Instituto Projeto Neymar Jr., for example. Located in Praia Grande, Brazil, this institute is Neymar's way of giving back to the community where he grew up. It's a place where kids can go to learn, play, and grow in a safe environment. The institute offers a range of educational and sporting programs, making sure kids get the chance to chase their dreams, just like Neymar did. It's not just a charity; it's a launchpad for the next generation of dreamers.

And Neymar's commitment to mentoring doesn't stop at his work with this charity. Back in the locker room and on the training grounds, he's also a mentor to the younger players. Stepping into a big club like PSG can be daunting for young talents, but Neymar, with his experience and understanding of the game, makes it a point to be there to guide them. He talks to them, trains with them, and shares tips that only someone with his experience could offer. He continually shows a commitment to passing on the wisdom he has picked up along the way, easing the pressure these young players are under, and reminding them that soccer, at its heart, is about joy, passion, and teamwork.

In all these roles, Neymary's influence at PSG and beyond is a testament to his versatility not just as a player but as a leader and a philanthropist. His ability to affect change, inspire younger players, and contribute to the community shows a side of Neymar that goes beyond what we see on match days. It's about impact—making a difference in every arena he steps into, whether it's the lush green pitch of Parc des Princes or the community fields back in Brazil. For Neymar, leadership is woven into his play, his public life, and his charitable efforts, creating a legacy that's about much more than just soccer.

Mbappé's Young Leadership and Participation in Community Service

While Kylian Mbappé is making defenders sweat on the pitch, off the pitch, he's also sprinting towards becoming a standout leader and a beacon of hope for many. Despite his young age, Mbappé isn't just playing the game; he's changing it, both inside and outside the stadium.

Imagine walking into the locker room, and there's Mbappé, with all his star power, yet he's one of the most approachable guys around. From day one at PSG, he's been not only a player but also a presence. You might think that being young and famous could go to someone's head, right? But that's exactly where Mbappé makes a striking difference from the expectations that hang over him. His approach is all about lifting others as he rises.

In the locker room, his influence is palpable. He's not just talking about passing balls; he's passing on wisdom, energy, and motivation. Even though he's younger or the same age as many of his teammates, they look up to him because he leads by example. Whether it's staying late after training to perfect his strikes or discussing play strategies, Mbappé's leadership style is about inspiring by doing. This kind of leadership is like a fresh breeze—subtle yet powerful—and it invigorates everyone to step up their game.

Now, let's zoom out of the locker room and into the community: Mbappé's heart is as big as his footwork is fast. He's deeply involved in community service, especially initiatives that uplift underprivileged kids in France. Imagine being a kid facing tough times and then finding out that Mbappé's in your corner. It's uplifting!

His commitment includes hefty donations and active participation in campaigns aimed at providing educational and sports opportunities to children who might otherwise miss out. Through these initiatives, Mbappé isn't just writing checks; he's crafting better, brighter futures for France's young people, giving kids the tools and chances they need to dream big and chase those dreams, just like he himself did.

Speaking of dreams, let's talk about how Mbappé is championing the cause of youth sports and education. It's no secret that sports can transform people's lives, teaching them values like teamwork, discipline, and resilience. Mbappé isn't just a poster boy for programs to give more people access to these benefits; he's a driving force behind them. He works with various organizations to promote sports participation among young people, not just as a path to becoming professional players but as a way to foster personal and social development. Through workshops, sports clinics, and public speaking events, Mbappé shares his journey and the lessons he's learned, emphasizing that the discipline, teamwork, and ethics learned on the field are skills that can help you win in life too.

Lastly, the impact of Mbappé's clean public image and how he carries himself is something that resonates worldwide. In a world where professional athletes often find themselves becoming infamous for their off-field antics, Mbappé stands out for his professionalism and demeanor. This makes him a role model not just for aspiring soccer players but for many young people. He shows that achieving greatness isn't just about what you do with the eyes of an audience on you; it's also about how you conduct yourself outside of the public sphere. His approachable personality, combined with his commitment to excellence and community, inspires young athletes around the globe to not only aim for excellence in their sport but also to be individuals of good character.

In essence, Mbappé's journey of young leadership and community involvement is a vivid illustration of how the lines between being a sports icon and a community leader can blur, creating a legacy that's about more than just goals scored or matches won. Our favorite soccer greats are all about impacting lives, inspiring change, and leading by example, both on and off the field. So, as you watch Mbappé blaze past defenders or smile for the cameras, remember that there's a lot more to this young star than meets the eye. He's not just playing the game; he's setting an example and paving the way for future generations, proving that true success is measured not just by your personal achievements but by the positive impact you have on others.

Haaland's Emerging Role as a Team Leader

Imagine stepping onto a soccer field, not just as a player but as a rising star whose job isn't only to score goals but also to lift the entire team's spirit and performance. Welcome to the world of Erling Haaland, whose leap into leadership at a young age has been as dynamic as his play on the field. From his early days, Haaland showed signs that he wasn't just another striker; he was a powerhouse of physical skill and emotional intelligence, ready to shoulder the responsibility of leading by example.

Think of Haaland as that one friend you play Fortnite with who not only knows all the best moves but also cheers you on as you pull off your own. On the field, he's the guy setting the pace, pushing forward, and always looking to create opportunities, not just for himself but for the team. His leadership style is all about showing how things are done. Whether it's through his rigorous training regimen, his focus during matches, or his never-say-die attitude, Haaland leads by showing up, every day, ready to give his all. This approach naturally lifts his team's morale; after all, when you see a leader giving their best, it's contagious—you want to step up your game too.

Now, let's consider how Haaland's unique playing style shapes team tactics: Have you heard about the way master chess players think five moves ahead? That's Haaland in soccer. His ability to read the game and make sharp on-field decisions influences his team's strategies significantly. Whether it's his positioning that opens up spaces for his teammates to collaborate and thrive or his physical presence that draws defenders and allows others to find opportunities, Haaland's impact is evident. His versatility means that coaches can flexibly adjust tactics, knowing they have a player who can adapt and excel in various formations, whether by leading the attack or pulling back slightly to link play.

The integration of new players is another arena where Haaland's versatility and kindness empower his whole team to shine. Joining a new team can be daunting, but having a teammate like Haaland can make it a whole lot smoother. Imagine it's your first day at a new school, and the coolest kid in class walks up and starts showing you around, making you feel welcome; not only that, they're there to help you laugh off and move on from any mishaps, as well as tell you which teachers are more generous with the hall pass. Haaland plays this part in the locker room. He's been noted for his role in helping new signings blend into the team dynamics, sharing insights about playing styles, guiding their understanding of team strategies, and easing their transition both on and off the field. This not only helps new players adjust quickly but also strengthens the team's cohesion and performance.

Haaland doesn't just influence people through how he plays or trains; he inspires those around him through his quick thinking and compassion both on and off the field. Consider those moments when the team is trailing, and the pressure is mounting. Then, Haaland does what he does best: breaks through and scores or makes that key pass leading to a goal. These moments are more than just game-changers; they're morale boosters, proving to his team that no matter the odds, they are never out of the game. His ability to perform under pressure and deliver when it matters most doesn't just win games; it builds belief within the team, fortifying their spirit and drive to succeed.

As Haaland continues to develop his leadership skills, his influence within the team is a powerful reminder of how leading by example and being a supportive teammate can elevate everyone's game. His journey demonstrates that leadership isn't just about wearing the captain's armband; it's about how you inspire, support, and push your team towards greatness in all aspects of their lives.

As we wrap up this exploration of leadership in soccer, it's clear the impact of the greats extends far beyond their goal-scoring ability. Through their dedication, adaptability, generosity, and supportive nature, they have built legacies of leadership that will continue to inspire not only future generations of players, or even solely fútbol fans, but a wide variety of people across the globe. As we move forward to dive deeper into these legacies in the next chapter, keep in mind the powerful role that a leader plays, not just in directing play on the pitch but also in crafting a team and community that believes, achieves, and excels together.

Chapter 7:

Legacy and Impact

Isn't it amazing how some soccer players not only dazzle us with their moves but also leave a lasting mark on the game itself? In this chapter, we're diving into how their legacies were made, and the soccer pitch is just the beginning. It's not just about what these legends do with the ball; it's about how they've changed the game of soccer forever. So, grab your favorite snack, and let's kick off this exciting chat with how Messi has not only played the game but reshaped it entirely!

Messi's Innovation in Playmaking and Dribbling Techniques

Revolutionizing Dribbling

Imagine being so good at moving with the soccer ball that it almost seems like it's connected to your feet with magnets. That's Messi for you! His dribbling is like watching a magic show; you never know what he's going to pull off next! "But what makes Messi's dribbling so special?" you ask. It's all about his low center of gravity. As we know, Messi is a bit shorter than most soccer giants, and he has turned this into his superpower. It allows him to zip and zoom around the field with the ball sticking close, making it super tough for defenders to catch him. It's like trying to grab a slippery fish with your bare hands—good luck with that!

Players all over the world watch Messi's games, not just for entertainment but to learn a trick or two. His dribbling style has become a textbook example in soccer coaching clinics globally. Coaches use clips of Messi's games to show young players how to keep control of the ball under pressure, change direction quickly, and use their body to shield the ball. It's like he's the professor of Dribbling 101, and everyone's eager to attend his class!

Creativity in Playmaking

Now, onto Messi's playmaking, which is as creative as a master painter with a blank canvas. His ability to see and make passes that no one else sees and to set up goals is what makes him a top-notch playmaker. Do you remember the many times that he has sliced through the defense with a perfect through-ball to set up a goal? It's like he has a GPS system in his brain that calculates the perfect route for the ball. Messi is a master composer on the pitch, and every pass and move he makes is perfectly orchestrated to create scoring opportunities.

His creativity makes everyone around him better. Players like Suarez and Neymar have thrived alongside him, partly because Messi knows exactly how to deliver the ball into spaces that maximize their chances of scoring. Every match is a chance for Messi to display more of his perfect passing prowess and create more goal-scoring masterpieces.

Influence on Youth Development Programs

Messi's style of play isn't just for the here and now, however; it's influencing how young players are being trained around the world. Youth academies from Barcelona to Beijing are teaching their players to emulate aspects of Messi's game. Coaches focus on developing players' abilities to control the ball tightly, make quick decisions, and find their teammates when everyone is moving at speed. It's like Messi has sparked a revolution in how soccer is taught at the grassroots level, emphasizing skill and creativity over mere physicality.

Enduring Impact on Fútbol Tactics

Lastly, let's talk about the long-term impact Messi has had on fútbol tactics. Teams have literally had to redesign their strategies to try and stop him. Some opt for crowding him with multiple defenders, while others try to cut off his passing lanes. Then, there are teams that just cross their fingers and hope for the best! His presence on the field has forced coaches to think creatively and adapt their tactics, often setting up their entire defensive strategy with Messi in mind.

Messi's influence on soccer tactics has been profound. He's forced teams to innovate and adapt, which, in turn, has led to a richer, more strategic game overall. It's like he's the final boss in a video game that everyone keeps trying to beat, but he's always one step ahead. His legacy in fútbol tactics will be talked about for generations, not just because he's a fantastic player but also because he's changed the way the game is played both at the highest levels and in local community games.

So, as we explore the twists and turns of Messi's impact on soccer, it's clear that his legacy is woven deeply into the fabric of the sport. From redefining dribbling to inspiring young players and reshaping fútbol tactics, Messi has left a permanent mark on the world of soccer. This shows us how one person's skill, vision, and creativity can ripple across fields and continents, influencing the game in countless ways. And who knows? Maybe, somewhere out there, a young player is practicing right now, ready to take the mantle and continue that legacy in their own unique way. Maybe, that person is you! The game never stops, and Messi's legacy lives on, one dribble, one play, at a time.

Ronaldo's Physicality and Longevity in Soccer

Hey, have you noticed how some soccer players seem to defy age, sprinting down the field like they've just started their careers? Well, Cristiano Ronaldo is like the poster boy for not letting a little thing like age slow you down. This guy's commitment to staying fit isn't just impressive; it's almost legendary. Imagine having the stamina of a teenager even when you're in your mid-30s, competing against players who could be your younger siblings. That's Ronaldo for you, and here's the scoop on how he's managed to keep rocking the soccer world with his fitness and agility.

Ronaldo's fitness regime is a master class in athleticism. He's not just hitting the gym and pumping iron. Nope, he's engaging with a carefully crafted wellness program that covers everything from high-intensity cardio to strength training and even a specific diet that is tailored to maximize his physical capabilities.

His workout sessions are the stuff of legend, involving not just routine exercises but also high-tech equipment to measure and enhance his muscle function, stamina, and recovery speed. This approach has set a new standard in the soccer world, showing that being fit isn't just about running on the pitch and avoiding injuries; it's about elevating your game to stay two steps ahead of the competition.

Now, think about this: Soccer careers tend to be pretty short, right? Most players have started to wind down by their early 30s, but not Ronaldo. His dedication to maintaining peak physical condition has allowed him to continue playing at the highest levels, challenging the traditional boundaries of a soccer player's career span.

Clubs and players worldwide have taken note, realizing that with the right care and training, their playing days don't have to be as numbered as they once thought. Ronaldo has essentially shifted the goalposts, showing that age is just a number if you're willing to put in the work to keep your body in top shape.

But Ronaldo's influence doesn't stop at pushing the boundaries of career lengths. His training plans have inspired clubs across the globe to rethink how they prepare their players. Many teams have started integrating similar routines, focusing more on holistic fitness programs that are tailored to individual players' needs rather than one-size-fits-all workouts.

These programs often include elements of Ronaldo's routine, like targeted strength training, personalized nutrition plans, and even mental health strategies to help players stay sharp both on and off the field. It's like Ronaldo has kick-started a fitness and well-being revolution in soccer, pushing teams to adopt more advanced and customized approaches to athlete health and training.

And let's not forget about the role model factor. For anyone dreaming of becoming the next big soccer star, Ronaldo's physicality and dedication to fitness are nothing short of inspiring. He's shown that being a top athlete isn't just about natural talent; it's about hard work, discipline, and a commitment to taking care of your body. For aspiring players, Ronaldo's routine offers a blueprint for how to prepare, perform, and persevere in sports. His influence extends beyond the professional realm, setting a new standard for young athletes everywhere on the importance of fitness in achieving and maintaining peak performance levels.

So, as we watch Ronaldo outmaneuver players half his age, remember, it's not just natural talent or experience at play. It's his revolutionary approach to physical fitness and mental wellness, an approach that has redefined what longevity in soccer can look like. Whether it's on the training ground or in a high-stakes match, Ronaldo's dedication to staying in top form continues to inspire, influence, and reshape the world of soccer, one powerful sprint at a time.

Neymar's Role in Popularizing Brazilian Flair Worldwide

Have you ever watched Neymar play? It's like he's dancing with the soccer ball at a carnival in Rio! This guy has taken the sizzling flair and jaw-dropping creativity of Brazilian culture and splashed it across the global soccer stage. Neymar is a one-man festival of skills and thrills, and his impact on the game stretches far beyond the goals he scores.

In fact, Neymar has become the global ambassador of Brazilian soccer. Imagine soccer as a language everyone can speak with different accents. Neymar's Brazilian accent is full of rhythm and dazzling moves, all at a high pace. This style is full of quick bursts of brilliance, and it takes a playful approach to facing challenges on the field.

This has not only captivated fans worldwide but also enhanced Brazil's legacy as a fútbol powerhouse. Wherever he plays, whether with Barcelona, Paris, or during international fixtures with Brazil, Neymar brings a piece of Brazilian culture with him, showcasing the beautiful game in a style that's uniquely Brazilian. It's like he invites everyone to a party where soccer is celebrated with every dribble, pass, and goal.

Because of this, and a variety of other factors, Neymar's playing style has influenced players and teams around the world. He has a knack for making the difficult look effortless. His quick feet, sharp mind, and flair for the dramatic have inspired a wave of players around the globe to incorporate more flair and skill into their own games.

Coaches in Europe, Asia, and America watch Neymar's games not just to get a feel for the skills of an opponent but to pick up tricks that might inject creativity and unpredictability into their own teams. It's as if Neymar is teaching a workshop on modern soccer, and the whole world is enrolled. You see young players trying to mimic his dribbles in London, imitate his samba style in Tokyo, and replicate his fearless attacking spirit in New York. Neymar has turned the soccer field into a global classroom where the curriculum is all about flair, creativity, and having the courage to express yourself.

Moving on to his marketing and media impact, Neymar's style and personality have a unique appeal that transcends the traditional boundaries of sports marketing. He isn't just selling soccer; he's selling a lifestyle. Whether it's his flashy celebrations, his trendsetting hairstyles, or his deep involvement in social media, Neymar knows how to keep the audience engaged and entertained.

Brands want to partner with him not only because he's a phenomenal soccer player but also because he connects with young people on a level that goes beyond the game. His social media posts attract millions of views, and his presence in advertisements can boost sales and viewership numbers overnight. As a result, Neymar doesn't just play in stadiums; he plays on every screen, in every household that follows soccer, making him a global icon in sports and beyond.

Lastly, let's shine a light on how Neymar inspires children in Brazil and around the world. Every kid playing soccer in the narrow streets of São Paulo or the sprawling fields of rural America looks up to him as a hero who plays with joy and an unbridled passion.

Neymar's journey from his humble beginnings in Santos to the glamorous spotlights of Paris serves as a beacon of hope and shows young people all over the globe where talent, dedication, and flair can take you. This makes him a powerful role model for millions of kids who dream of dribbling past life's obstacles with a smile. In Neymar, they see a reflection of what they can achieve, not just in terms of soccer skills but in embracing their heritage and projecting it onto the world stage with pride and confidence.

Through his global ambassadorship, influential playing style, and charismatic presence, Neymar continues to weave the rich tapestry of Brazilian soccer into the fabric of global sports culture. His impact resonates in the cheers of the stadiums, the practices of budding soccer players, and the strategies of coaches worldwide, proving that the essence of Brazilian soccer—its flair, joy, and artistry—is universal. Neymar has transformed the game, inviting everyone to savor the Brazilian flavor of soccer.

Mbappé's Influence on Young French Athletes

Kylian Mbappé is one of those people who are so cool and talented that they make everything seem possible. He's a soccer sensation who's not just lighting up the fields in France but also setting an example and providing inspiration that's sweeping across the globe as quickly as his lightning-fast sprints.

Mbappé was "just" a young kid from Bondy, but now, he's dribbling his way through life's challenges to become one of the world's most celebrated athletes. He shows us time and time again that anything is possible. This is particularly true because he's not just a star on the field; he's a beacon of hope and a source of inspiration—especially for young athletes all across France—showing that with enough grit and determination, the sky's the limit.

Mbappé's journey resonates so deeply with young French athletes because his story began in a regular suburban neighborhood, just like theirs. This makes him a role model for any sporty kid, regardless of whether they play soccer or not. He's shown that it doesn't matter where you come from; what matters is where you're going.

For kids hitting the local fields, practicing in tiny gyms, or sprinting on worn-out tracks, Mbappé's success is evidence that dreams can come true and, yes, hard work really does pay off. His dedication, discipline, and relentless pursuit of excellence are the perfect playbook for any young athlete dreaming of making it big. He's a real-life example of how hard work, not just talent, crafts champions.

But his influence doesn't stop there. Let's talk about the impact of this young legend on French soccer culture. Mbappé's rise has been a jolt of energy to the heart of French fútbol. In the 2018 World Cup, Mbappé helped France clinch the trophy, and it wasn't just a victory for the team; it was a revitalizing boost for the entire country's soccer scene.

His dynamic play, fearless attitude, and youthful charisma have empowered Mbappé to inject new life into the national league and team. Stadiums are buzzing, jerseys are selling out, and more kids are signing up to play soccer. Mbappé has reminded everyone of the magic and passion that soccer brings, rekindling a love for the game that seemed to be simmering on the back burner.

Additionally, his involvement in community and youth programs across France shows that he's serious about lifting others as he climbs. From visiting schools to participating in charity matches, Mbappé is often seen giving back to the community. He invests his time and resources in helping young athletes find their footing.

These initiatives are about more than just teaching soccer skills; they instill confidence, discipline, and a sense of responsibility in many young people. Imagine being a young soccer player, and there's Mbappé, not on a poster but right there, in your community, talking about his experiences, sharing tips, and maybe even kicking the ball around. It's this level of involvement that endears him to many, making him a role model who's accessible and real.

Lastly, let's not overlook how Mbappé, with his African heritage, stands as a proud symbol of diversity and success in modern France. His rise to stardom from a diverse suburb reflects the multicultural melting pot of the country and highlights the potential that lies in its diverse population.

Mbappé's success story is especially powerful when seen against the backdrop of ongoing discussions about integration and representation in sports and society at large. In this regard, he's not just a soccer player; he's a symbol of what France is and what it can be: diverse, dynamic, and successful on the world stage. For many young people—in particular those from minority backgrounds—Mbappé is a figure of hope, signaling that their dreams are valid and achievable.

In essence, Mbappé's influence on young athletes in France extends far beyond his goals on the field. He is a role model, a community leader, and a beacon of diversity and success, inspiring a new generation to chase their dreams with the same fervor and passion he shows every time he steps on the pitch. As these young athletes lace up their boots, whether on a small field in Marseille or in a big arena in Lyon, they carry with them the inspiration that Mbappé imparts: Dream big, work hard, and never forget where you came from.

Haaland's New Era of Forwards and Role Model Status

Erling Haaland is redefining what it means to be a forward in soccer. He expertly combines the speed of a sprinter, the size of a basketball player, and the technical skills of a top-class fútbol player. Haaland's changing how the striker position is seen worldwide.

Picture this: You're a defender, and you see Haaland charging towards you—yikes, right? His ability to outrun defenders while controlling the ball flawlessly is setting new standards for what teams expect from their forwards. It's like he's built for soccer's future, fast-paced and super skilled.

Now, let's zoom out a bit and see how Haaland's style is shaking up the soccer world beyond just the matches he plays in. Clubs all over the globe are taking notes and scrambling to find their own version of Haaland. Scouts are on the lookout for players who not only have the physicality to overpower defenders but also the speed to break away and the skills to finish plays.

Haaland has sparked a gold rush in the soccer scouting world, with teams eager to discover young players who can emulate his powerful yet technical style of play. This shift is influencing youth academies too, where training programs are increasingly focusing on developing well-rounded forwards who can do it all—run, shoot, and score—just like Haaland.

But as with our other legends, Haaland's influence isn't just about how he plays; it's also about how he carries himself both on and off the field. As he is known for his sportsmanship and professionalism, Haaland is setting the bar high for how soccer stars should act.

Whether he's playing a tough match or interacting with fans, Haaland remains humble and respectful, showing that being a good sport is as important as scoring goals. This attitude is especially refreshing in today's competitive sports environment, where pressure can sometimes lead to heated moments. Young players watching Haaland can learn that you can be one of the best in the game and still maintain great sportsmanship. He's a true class act!

And speaking of inspiring the next generation, Haaland's part as a role model—particularly back home in Norway—is something that really stands out when we consider his legacy. Coming from a country that's not traditionally known as a soccer powerhouse, Haaland's rise to international stardom is like a script from an inspiring sports movie.

For kids in Norway and nations not known for fútbol everywhere, he's living proof that where you come from doesn't limit where you can go. Haaland shows that with enough talent, determination, and hard work, reaching the world stage is totally possible. This makes him a symbol of hope and a source of national pride, inspiring kids to dream big and chase those dreams with all they've got.

So, as we chat about Haaland's impact, it's clear he's more than just a goal-scoring machine. He's a trendsetter in soccer tactics, a role model in sportsmanship, and an inspiration to aspiring players around the globe. Through his breathtaking skills and commendable demeanor, Haaland is not just carving out a stellar career for himself; he's also shaping the future of soccer, showing us all how the beautiful game should be played: with speed, strength, skill, and a whole lot of heart.

As we wrap up this exciting chat about Haaland, remember that his story is still being written. Every match is a chance to see this soccer phenomenon push the limits of what forwards can do, both on the pitch and in the wider sports culture. Keep watching, keep cheering, and who knows? Maybe, the next soccer revolution is just a kick away, inspired by none other than Erling Haaland himself.

Never forget that the legends of fútbol have built legacies that rest on more than their amazing skills. Being a world-class player involves a lot of heart too. From revolutionizing forms of play to reinvesting in their communities, the superstars of soccer change both the game and the world with their well-rounded approaches to life. Now, let's gear up and move to our next adventure in the world of soccer.

Chapter 8:

The Future of Soccer

Hey there, soccer fans and future stars! Have you ever wondered what happens when legends of the game hang up their boots? Well, stick around because we're about to dive into the world of what comes next. What if the magician on the field could transform into a wizard on the sidelines? Intrigued? Let's begin by exploring the possibilities that await Messi as he considers hanging up his boots and maybe swapping them for a coach's whistle.

Messi's Transition Into Retirement and Potential Coaching

End of Playing Career

Picture this: The stadium is packed, fans are chanting, and there's Messi, dribbling down the pitch for perhaps the last time. It's an emotional roller coaster, right? As Messi approaches the inevitable decision of retirement, several factors come into play. It's not just about how his legs feel or how many goals he's still scoring; it's about timing and the desire to leave at the top of his game. Messi has always been one to dazzle on the field, so the thought of him stepping away might seem a bit surreal. However, even soccer legends have to think about their final whistle. For Messi, his considerations include his physical condition, family desires, and the chance to leave a lasting legacy while still at the peak of his powers, but the most important part for him is being able to support his team effectively. He has said, "I know that as soon as I believe that I can no longer perform, or no longer enjoy the game, or not [be] able to help my teammates, then I will stop" (Millar, 2024).

Transition to Coaching

Perhaps, Messi could swap his soccer kit for a coach's cap. Imagine him on the sidelines, his intense gaze following every pass and every run. Coaching would be a fantastic next chapter for him, given his profound understanding of the game and natural leadership abilities. Messi has a mind that sees soccer plays unfold like a grandmaster in chess. This insight could tremendously benefit young players, shaping their careers just as his was shaped by greats before him. Picture him guiding the next generation, sharing the secrets of those mesmerizing dribbles and game-changing plays. Coaching would not only keep Messi connected with the sport he loves but also amplify his impact by molding future stars.

Legacy Preservation

Moving from the pitch to the dugout could indeed be a game-changer for Messi's legacy. It would allow him to pass the torch to a whole new generation of players by turning his years of experience into lessons that can elevate them. By stepping into a coaching role, Messi could extend his influence in soccer far beyond his playing days. It's one thing to be remembered as a phenomenal player, but becoming a great coach could cement a legacy that would echo through the ages. Messi's potential shift to coaching could inspire players to think about the game differently and play with heart, intelligence, and that magical Messi flair.

Impact on Fútbol Tactics

Messi's deep tactical knowledge could also bring fresh ideas to soccer coaching. He has not only played under some of the best coaches in the world but he's also been a tactical genius on the field. His ability to read the game and find spaces where no one else can could lead to innovative playing styles and strategies, potentially changing how many teams play. Imagine teams employing the "Messi method"— a blend of strategic foresight and creative freedom on the field, all from the mind of one of the greatest players ever.

So, as we explore the possibilities of Messi's future in soccer, it's clear that his retirement from playing could just be the beginning of an exciting new chapter. Whether he's orchestrating match-winning plays from the sidelines or developing the potential of young talents, Messi's influence on soccer is set to continue, just in a different role. For now, we can only wait and see where the next part of his soccer journey takes him, but one thing is for certain: The Messi magic isn't disappearing; it's merely transforming.

Ronaldo's Business Ventures and Soccer Academies

Cristiano Ronaldo is not just shaping the future of the sport; he's building a worldwide legacy of excellence! Beyond his breathtaking goals and jaw-dropping plays, Ronaldo is diving headfirst into the world of business and soccer development. It's like he's playing a whole new game, but this time he's working his magic off the field, and trust me, it's just as exciting!

Entrepreneurial Pursuits

Let's kick things off with Ronaldo's ventures in the fashion and lifestyle arena. Imagine this: You've just scored a goal, and you want to look as sharp off the field as you performed on it. Who you gonna call? Ronaldo, of course! With his own fashion line, he's bringing the same elegance and flair that he shows on the field to his lines of clothing and accessories.

But Ronaldo's business interests don't stop at fashion. He's also got his own hotels, which are about as luxurious as you'd expect from a fútbol superstar. These ventures are about more than just making money; they're creating a brand that embodies excellence, style, and the high standards Ronaldo is known for. So, whether you're wearing his designs or staying at one of his hotels, you're experiencing a piece of the Ronaldo magic.

Development of Soccer Academies

Young soccer players with dreams as big as Ronaldo's goals are also having their lives changed by his legacy. Where do they go to make their dreams a reality? Ronaldo's soccer academies, of course! These are a breeding ground for future champions, molded in the ethos of Ronaldo's own journey and values. Here, it's not just about learning to kick a ball; it's about nurturing talent, dedication, and the mental toughness required to excel at the highest levels. Ronaldo's vision for these academies is clear: to give back to the community by providing kids with opportunities to rise through the ranks, just like he did. He's all about creating pathways for young talents who might otherwise never get the chance to shine, turning potential into excellence.

Global Soccer Influence

But Ronaldo's influence stretches far beyond his local community. His academies have a global reach, impacting young lives in different corners of the world. Imagine a kid in a remote village, playing soccer barefoot, who suddenly gets the chance to train at a state-of-the-art Ronaldo academy. That's the kind of global impact we're talking about. These academies instill a global standard of training, discipline, and professionalism, and the ripple effect is massive, changing the landscape of youth soccer development worldwide. By bringing top-tier training and facilities to underserved regions, Ronaldo is helping to level the playing field, giving every young player a fighting chance to pursue their soccer dreams.

Brand Legacy

Lastly, let's chat about how all these ventures contribute to Ronaldo's overall brand legacy. He won't just be remembered as a great player but as a visionary who reshaped the future of soccer both on and off the field. Through his many ventures, Ronaldo is building a legacy that will last well beyond his playing days.

Each business and academy is a piece of his ambition, crafted to ensure that his impact on the world continues to grow. He's creating lasting connections with fans, inspiring the next generation, and leaving a mark that extends beyond goals and championships. Ronaldo's brand is synonymous with excellence, and every venture he undertakes reinforces this message, ensuring that his influence will be felt for generations to come.

So, as we explore Ronaldo's off-field gameplay, it's clear he's not just planning on sitting back and relaxing when he retires entirely. He's actively shaping his legacy, ensuring that his impact resonates not just through his achievements but through his ongoing contributions to the sport and society.

Whether it's through the stylish offerings of his brand or the transformative education at his academies, Ronaldo is setting the stage for a future where his legacy continues to inspire and elevate the beautiful game. As budding soccer fans and players, you're not just witnessing the tail end of a stellar career; you're watching the evolution of a soccer legend into a global icon whose influence extends far beyond the pitch and molds the future of soccer in exciting and enduring ways.

Neymar's Plans Beyond PSG and His Brand Legacy

Have you ever wondered what a soccer superstar like Neymar does after dazzling fans in Paris? Well, grab your passport because we might be taking a trip to, well, just about anywhere! That's right, Neymar's future could be as packed with surprises as his plays on the pitch.

After Neymar's stint with Paris Saint-Germain, the world will be his oyster. Could he return to Brazil to bring his career full circle? Or perhaps, a new league is calling his name, offering fresh challenges and adventures. Imagine Neymar lighting up stadiums in the United States or even adding some samba flair to a club in Japan! The possibilities are as exciting as a last-minute penalty kick.

But Neymar is also a master of branding. Think of him as not just a player but a full-on lifestyle influencer. With his knack for entertainment and fashion, Neymar's brand is as vibrant and dynamic as his footwork. He isn't just slapping his name on a sports drink or other fad product; we're talking about major partnerships with international companies that align with his flashy, fun-loving personality.

Whether it's launching his own line of fragrances or collaborating with a big-time fashion house, Neymar knows how to make a splash. And let's not forget the digital world! With his massive social media following, Neymar connects with fans worldwide, sharing not just soccer skills but also snippets of his glamorous life, making his personal brand one of the most recognized and beloved around.

But something that truly showcases the size of Neymar's heart is his commitment to charitable efforts. Neymar isn't just about scoring goals on the pitch; he's also helping others to make their own personal goals happen through his charity work. As we learned in the last chapter, his institute in Brazil has been a game-changer, offering education and sports programs to children, helping them to play their way to brighter futures.

But Neymar's vision for the future goes beyond local boundaries. His aim is to expand these philanthropic efforts even further on a global scale, reaching out to underprivileged kids all around the world. Imagine a larger network of Neymar-supported schools and programs, each sparking dreams and offering opportunities for kids, from Rio de Janeiro to rural Kenya. Neymar is all about using his spotlight to shine a light on those in need, proving that soccer can be a force for good.

Lastly, let's talk about Neymar's continuing impact back home in Brazil. Even when playing matches leagues away, his influence on Brazilian fútbol remains unmatched. As a role model, Neymar keeps on inspiring legions of young players who see in him the dreams they wish to chase, and this will be his largest impact for the foreseeable future.

His flair, combined with his success, tells a compelling story of what's possible with talent and determination. By possibly returning to play in Brazil or even just getting more involved in Brazilian soccer development, Neymar could help elevate the local leagues there and nurture the next generation of Brazilian stars. His presence alone boosts interest, draws crowds, and generates buzz, helping to grow the sport in his home country. As we watch his influence grow even more, we'll undoubtedly keep seeing him give back to the place that shaped him and, in doing so, shape the future of the sport there as well.

So, as Neymar contemplates his next moves, both on and off the field, his potential to influence soccer and society remains as dynamic as ever. From dazzling us with his skills in new leagues to expanding his business empire and boosting his charitable initiatives, Neymar is set to keep making waves. And through it all, his love for the game and his desire to give back promise to keep his growing legacy vibrant and impactful, spreading joy and inspiration both on the pitch and beyond. Whether he's breaking records with his dribbles or breaking barriers with his charity work, Neymar's journey continues to be one to watch, full of potential and promise for exciting new chapters.

Mbappé's Prospects for Ballon d'Or and Future Leagues

Kylian Mbappé is a name that echoes in the realms of fútbol like a thunderclap on a clear day. He's a comet blazing through the skies of soccer greatness. Now, let's zoom into the future a bit. Imagine Mbappé lifting the prestigious Ballon d'Or. Sounds exciting, right? Well, it's not that far-fetched an idea! Given his meteoric rise to success and the sheer talent he displays on the pitch, Mbappé is already on the radar for this well-known award.

But snagging the Ballon d'Or requires more than just scoring hat tricks or dazzling with dribbles; it's about consistency at the highest level, making key plays in crucial moments, and staying at the peak of your game throughout the season. For

Mbappé, this means keeping his engines firing on all cylinders, not just in domestic leagues but also by lighting up the Champions League and international tournaments. Every match is a step, every goal a leap, toward that golden trophy.

Now, let's play with the idea of Mbappé exploring new horizons—perhaps, a new league. Mbappé, with his lightning speed and killer instincts, could be taking on defenders in the English Premier League or outsmarting tacticians in the Serie A in the future. Exciting, isn't it?

Each league has its own flavor, rhythm, and challenges. So, moving to a new league would not only test Mbappé's adaptability but also enhance his skills and marketability. Imagine the buzz, the posters, the headlines: "Mbappé takes on a new challenge!" He'll be adding new chapters to his already thrilling story, broadening his horizons, and of course, sending his fan jerseys flying off the shelves across the globe.

But here's where it gets even more interesting: What's Mbappé's plan for the long haul? Think about it; fútbol careers can be as unpredictable as lottery numbers. One minute you're up, the next you might be sidelined. For Mbappé, managing his physical health is crucial. This means not just training hard but training smart—understanding his body, knowing when to push and when to pause. It's about staying fit, staying agile, and most importantly, staying injury-free.

Moreover, adapting his game as he matures is key. As defenders get wiser to his tricks, Mbappé will need to evolve. Maybe, he'll use less sprinting and more strategic positioning, or perhaps, he'll focus on picking the perfect moment to strike rather than relying solely on speed.

Lastly, let's think about his growing legacy. How does Mbappé want to be remembered? What impact does he want to make—on the field and off it? Mbappé seems to be on a path to not just soccer stardom but also becoming a powerhouse of inspiration.

Whether it's through his philanthropic efforts, his demeanor on the field, or his connection with fans, Mbappé is crafting a legacy that might one day stand alongside the likes of Pelé and Maradona. He's a role model—a hero that kids will look up to, not just in France but around the world. Every dribble, every goal, and every gesture of sportsmanship is a brushstroke in the masterpiece of his career.

As we imagine all these possibilities, it's clear that Mbappé's future in fútbol holds as much excitement and potential as his play. Whether chasing the Ballon d'Or, dazzling in new leagues, or planning for a long and impactful career, Mbappé's journey in fútbol is shaping up to be one for the history books. And for us fans, it's a thrill to watch, a story to follow, and perhaps, a glimpse into the future of fútbol. So, keep your eyes on the pitch; Kylian Mbappé is not done surprising us yet.

Haaland's Expected Career Moves and Market Influence

Have you ever seen a soccer player so good that every club in the galaxy might want a piece of the action? Well, that's Erling Haaland for you! With his meteoric rise in the soccer world, we're watching a superstar in the making, and let me tell you, the future looks as bright as his goal-scoring record.

If we try to guess where this shooting star might land next, we might imagine Haaland—with his killer instincts and unmatched speed—joining a top club like Real Madrid or maybe even making a splash in the English Premier League. Clubs like these aren't just after his ability to smash goals but also his potential to lift trophies and bring that winning spirit to their squad.

But it's not just about which jersey he'll wear next. Every move Haaland makes can stir up the soccer market like a smoothie blender. Think about it; transferring a player of Haaland's caliber can shake things up, setting new benchmarks for transfer fees and salary structures. Clubs are on their toes, ready to break their piggy banks to have Haaland lead their line. His moves could push other clubs to up their game, not just on the field but in their financial strategies, ensuring they're not left behind in the race for top talent.

Switching gears to Haaland's marketability, boy, is it skyrocketing or what? With every goal, his face is becoming as famous as any celebrity out there. We're talking endorsements, brand deals, and maybe even his own line of sportswear. Companies are lining up, hoping to associate with Haaland's image of youth, vigor, and success. It's like everything he touches turns to marketing gold. From sports clothing to video games, having Haaland on board is guaranteed to boost sales and visibility. He's not just playing soccer, after all; he's shaping how soccer stars influence markets and trends.

Haaland is also a global soccer ambassador. With his charm and skills, he's perfectly poised to promote soccer in corners of the world where the sport is still catching up. Places where kids kick makeshift balls in dusty backyards could soon be buzzing with the excitement of soccer, all thanks to Haaland's influence. He has the power to inspire a new generation, showing them that with hard work and passion, reaching for the stars isn't just a dream but a very achievable reality. Haaland's global appeal could bring more attention, investment, and infrastructure to developing soccer markets, making the sport truly global.

So, as we watch Haaland sprint down the pitch, remember that his impact goes beyond goal records and match-winning performances. It's about setting new standards, inspiring young fans, and changing soccer, one thunderous goal at a time. Keep your eyes on this one, folks; he's on his way to becoming a legend, not just in the record books but in the hearts of soccer fans around the world.

Conclusion

Hey there, young champions! As we've journeyed together through the incredible stories of Lionel Messi, Cristiano Ronaldo, Neymar Júnior, Kylian Mbappé, and Erling Haaland, we've seen more than just fancy footwork and jaw-dropping goals; we've walked alongside these legends from their humble beginnings to the dizzying heights of global stardom. We've watched them transform from young talents into icons whose influence reaches far beyond the soccer field.

These players teach us the power of perseverance. Each of them faced challenges that could have sidelined their dreams. Yet, like true champions, they bounced back stronger, showing us that obstacles are just opportunities in disguise. They've adapted to new teams, countries, and styles of play, proving that being flexible and open to change is crucial, not just in soccer but in life.

Their leadership on and off the pitch has sparked changes in how teams operate and how young players are trained. But their impact isn't confined to tactics and trophies. These stars have used their fame to give back, contributing to charity causes and youth development, reshaping global soccer culture. We have clearly seen that these legends are not just players; they're builders of the future, helping to mold the next generation of soccer lovers and leaders.

Looking ahead, the legacies of Messi, Ronaldo, Neymar, Mbappé, and Haaland are set to grow even richer. Whether stepping into coaching roles, expanding their entrepreneurial ventures, or advocating for sports education, their paths will continue to inspire millions around the world, even when they decide to hang up their boots. They've shown that with talent, dedication, and heart, the possibilities are endless.

From my own perspective as someone passionate about guiding young souls like you in overcoming doubts and chasing dreams, these stories are goldmines of motivation. They're proof that no matter where you start, with hard work and belief, you can reach the stars. They also highlight the importance of mentorship and resilience—themes that resonate deeply with anyone striving to make a mark in any field.

So, what can you take from all this? **The journeys of these soccer legends not only celebrate their achievements on the field but also underscore the profound impact they have on society, inspiring every one of us to pursue excellence with integrity and passion.** Whether you're shooting goals, acing tests, or standing up for what's right, remember the lessons these icons have shared through their lives. And most importantly, never stop playing, learning, and dreaming.

As we wrap up, I want to remind you that soccer is more than just a game. It's a global language that speaks of unity, teaches life lessons, and brings joy to billions. It's a dance of cultures, a celebration of teamwork, and evidence of the power of the human spirit and our capacity for creativity. So, lace up your boots and hit the field, or simply cheer from the stands, but no matter what, be part of this beautiful game and carry its spirit wherever you go.

Keep playing, keep dreaming, and who knows? Maybe one day, I'll be writing about your legendary journey in the world of soccer. Until then, play on and aim high. Your goals are closer than they seem!

Keep kicking!

References

Academies - Santos: Neymar, the making of a star. (n.d.). FIFA. https://www.fifa.com/en/articles/academies-santos-neymar-the-making-of-a-star

Adler, N. (2022, November 30). *How immigration "made French football better."* Al Jazeera. https://www.aljazeera.com/news/2022/11/30/how-immigration-made-french-football-better

AllAttack. (2022, October 22). *The 15 best Neymar skill moves* [Video]. YouTube. https://www.youtube.com/watch?v=9GaFRZd8FsU

Butler, A. (2023, February 18). *Cristiano Ronaldo's rags to impossible riches.* Mail Online. https://www.dailymail.co.uk/sport/uk-sport-weekend-features-project/article-11763611/Cristiano-Ronaldos-rags-impossible-riches.html

Campbell, J. (2024, February 6). *From Senegal to Barcelona: Is Eyeball revolutionising global youth scouting?* The New York Times. https://www.nytimes.com/athletic/5229418/2024/02/06/from-senegal-to-barcelona-is-eyeball-revolutionising-global-youth-scouting/

Carey, M. (2023, October 19). *How the growth of wearable technology is transforming football.* The New York Times. https://www.nytimes.com/athletic/4966509/2023/10/19/wearable-technology-in-football/

Cristiano Ronaldo: From poverty to family and football superstardom. (n.d). SPYSCAPE. https://spyscape.com/article/cristiano-ronaldo-from-poverty-to-family-and-football-superstardom

Daly, C. (2023, July 8). *Inside Lionel Messi's personal life ahead of Inter Miami move.* Mail Online. https://www.dailymail.co.uk/sport/football/article-12265921/Lionel-Messis-personal-life-Married-holidays-Suarez-9m-Miami-apartment.html

Davey, L. (2024, May 16). *Ronaldo above Messi and Mbappé on rich list but hotel plan could widen gap.* TalkSPORT. https://talksport.com/football/1870895/cristiano-ronaldo-lionel-messi-kylian-mbappe-georgina-rodriguez-rich-list-luxury-hotel-plan/

Dawson, R. (2024, January 30). *Haaland set for City return after two months.* ESPN. https://www.espn.com/soccer/story/_/id/39420822/haaland-set-city-return-two-month-injury-guardiola

Doig, S. (2023, June 23). *Welcome to a new era of "footballer style."* The Telegraph. https://www.telegraph.co.uk/fashion/style/style-icon-erling-haaland-welcome-to-footballer-style/

Donica, A., & Piccotti, T. (2022, February 17). *Lionel Messi - Stats, family & facts.* Biography. https://www.biography.com/athletes/lionel-messi

Edgley, R. (2015, March 6). *The sports science behind Lionel Messi's amazing dribbling ability.* Bleacher Report. https://bleacherreport.com/articles/2375473-the-sports-science-behind-lionel-messis-amazing-dribbling-ability

Football - South American teams, rules, history. (n.d.). In *Encyclopædia Britannica.* https://www.britannica.com/sports/football-soccer/South-America

Goltsman, M. (2023, June 20). *The spectator effect: Psychological impact of audience presence on athletes.* Medium. https://mishagoltsman.medium.com/the-spectator-effect-psychological-impact-of-audience-presence-on-athletes-bd5a812effbe

Klosok, A., & Ramsay, G. (2020, September 15). *Neymar says he "acted like a fool" in brawl but demands racism must stop.* CNN. https://edition.cnn.com/2020/09/14/football/neymar-psg-marseille-racism-ligue-1-spt-intl/index.html

Kylian Mbappé and Erling Haaland in the Champions League. (2024, May 6). UEFA. https://www.uefa.com/uefachampionsleague/news/0266-1199ef3658d5-145c6798f795-1000--kylian-mbappe-and-erling-haaland-in-the-champions-league-sta/

Kylian Mbappé soccer speed workout. (n.d.). OvertimeAthletes. https://blog.overtimeathletes.com/kylian-mbappe-speed-workout/

Leadership lessons from Messi and Ronaldo. (2022, December 15). LeAP; Emids. https://leap.emids.com/leadership-lessons-from-messi-and-ronaldo/

Livie, A. (2023, November 7). *Erling Haaland "has done everything he could" to beat Lionel Messi and Kylian Mbappé to Ballon d'Or - Rio Ferdinand.* TNT Sports. https://www.tntsports.co.uk/football/champions-league/2022-2023/erling-haaland-has-done-everything-he-could-to-beat-lionel-messi-and-kylian-mbappe-to-ballon-d-or-ri_sto9874312/story.shtml

Messi was diagnosed with a growth disorder when he was 11. (2022, December 19). Moneycontrol. https://www.moneycontrol.com/news/trends/messi-was-diagnosed-with-a-growth-disorder-when-he-was-11-how-he-overcame-it-9729001.html

Millar, C. (2024, March 27). *Lionel Messi addresses retirement talk: "If I feel good, I will keep playing."* New York Times. https://www.nytimes.com/athletic/5372107/2024/03/27/lionel-messi-inter-miami-retirement/

The most charitable footballers in the world are also some of the most talented. (2024, June 12). Gameday News.

https://www.gamedaynews.com/soccer/the-most-charitable-footballers-in-the-world-are-also-some-of-the-most-talented/

Reardon, L. (2022, November 22). *5 things to know about 2018 World Cup champion Kylian Mbappé.* NBC 6 South Florida; NBCUniversal Media. https://www.nbcmiami.com/news/sports/world-cup-2022/5-things-to-know-about-2018-world-cup-champion-kylian-mbappe/2914860/

Smith, L. (2021, February 13). *The impact of social media on youth athletes.* Stack Sports. https://www.stack.com/a/the-impact-of-social-media-on-youth-athletes/

Soccer: A unifying force. (2024, January 2). Sogility. https://sogility.net/2024/01/soccer-a-unifying-force/

Staunton, P. (n.d.). *Messi and Ronaldo: Changing the face of football.* Goal. https://www.goal.com/story/messi-ronaldo-changing-face-of-football/index.html

Telseth, F., & Halldorsson, V. (2017). *The success culture of Nordic football: the cases of the national men's teams of Norway in the 1990s and Iceland in the 2010s.* Sport in Society, 22(4), 689–703. https://doi.org/10.1080/17430437.2017.1390928

University of Maryland. (2024, February 14). *Sports psychology: Unlocking mental resilience for peak performance.* https://health.umms.org/2024/02/14/sports-psychology/

Watch all of Lionel Messi's Champions League goals [Video]. (2020, August 27). UEFA. https://www.uefa.com/uefachampionsleague/history/video/0260-103b0d78a03d-df48aacb8349-1000--watch-all-of-lionel-messi-s-champions-league-goals/

When Neymar met Messi | 10 great Club World Cup moments. (2023, January 24). FIFA. https://www.fifa.com/en/articles/article-greater-than-fcwc-2022-greater-than-8-dtg-when-messi-met-neymar

Wikipedia. (n.d.). *List of career achievements by Cristiano Ronaldo.* https://en.wikipedia.org/wiki/List_of_career_achievements_b y_Cristiano_Ronaldo

Made in the USA
Coppell, TX
03 November 2024

39543954R00069